# LONDON'S

# *Historic Inns and Taverns*

# LONDON'S

# *Historic Inns and Taverns*

DONALD STUART

breedon **books**
PUBLISHING

First published in Great Britain in 2004 by
The Breedon Books Publishing Company Limited
Breedon House, 3 The Parker Centre,
Derby, DE21 4SZ.

ISBN 1 85983 398 5

Printed and bound by Scotprint,
Haddington, Scotland.

# CONTENTS

# *Chapter 1*
# PUB THEATRES

OVER the centuries playwrights have given shows in pubs and pub courtyards and for over 30 years some London pubs have set aside rooms for theatres. Some say the most exciting thing about such theatres is the intimacy between actors and audience, who are in such close proximity. Here are dramas, comedies, revival plays and musicals. Three centuries ago actors hired pubs and shops in central London to give recitals, hoping to catch the eye of theatre managers and thus gain further advancement in their careers.

Gatehouse (see p.11).

## BRIDGE HOUSE, Delamere Terrace, W2

Built in the early 1800s, this is an elegant building opposite the Grand Union Canal that houses the Canal Café Theatre. It has been a leading pub theatre for many years and Edinburgh Festival acts are previewed here. The bar is most

theatrical with elegant chandelier lighting and square, red, lantern-style light boxes. Nearby is the Puppet Theatre Barge. The canal was built in the 18th century for freight and paying passengers and the pub was used to house navigators and bargees. Now it is no longer a trade route but is used by walkers, anglers and pleasure boaters. It is also an important green corridor for wildlife in north London and narrowboats still use the original mile posts.

## BROCKLEY JACK, Brockley Road, SE4

Built on the site of the old Brockley Castle, there was another pub in this location before Brockley Jack opened in 1898. It is a rambling pub with a theatre behind the bar and over the entrance hangs part of the shoulder blade of a whale. A landlord here was a highwayman in his spare time, and just before being arrested he hanged himself

upstairs. His apparition seems to be still about as many have felt cold chills and his ghostly fingers on their person. Brockley Jack, real name Jack Camp, now features on the pub sign wearing the uniform of his second job. There was a village called Brocele near here as early as 1182, and the name meant a woodland clearing inhabited by a man called Broca, with a sett of badgers.

## CURTAIN'S UP, Comeragh Road, W14

Set on a corner among Georgian houses, the Curtain's Up has had a theatre for 12 years. Originally the Baron's Court Tavern, then the Baron's Ale House, the décor reflects the theatrical connection with masks and posters. The theatre is in the cellar with 60 seats around the stage on three sides and a small, square playing area. Sometimes this stage is extended into the playgoers area, and both classics and new works by unknown dramatists are performed.

## DRAYTON COURT, The Avenue, W13

This impressive pub has Gothic towers and a retinue of ghosts befitting its structure. Tales are told of lights going on and off without explanation and shadowy figures seen in corners. Once an hotel, it is now home to a well-known pub theatre and several bars. Outside is a wrought-iron terrace and

gardens. Decorating the walls are woodcut prints and a reproduction of the Bayeux Tapestry. It provides interesting and contemporary theatre in west London.

## GATEHOUSE, Highgate Hill, N6

Built in 1306, this was a pub for drovers bringing cattle and sheep to Smithfield Market, but the first official date on record is 1670, when a licensing application was made. It is set in the middle of the road on Highgate Hill. The auditorium, now the theatre, opened in 1865 for 'Balls, Cinderellas

and Concerts' and has been a music hall, cinema, Masonic Lodge and a venue for amateur dramatics. As the highest pub in London at 426 feet above sea level it is known as 'London's Top Theatre'. In 1905 it was renovated in the mock-Tudor style that it retains to this day. A dummy cupboard exists where Dick Turpin was able to hide to escape pursuers. The pub is haunted by Martha, or Mother Marnes, a former landlady murdered for her money. She often appears in the oldest part of the inn, along with her cat, dressed in black with a lace bonnet. Some have also seen a white-haired gentleman reflected in the mirrors wearing sea-going clothing and staring at the back of their heads. It has been a courtroom, and once had a rope running through it dividing the county of Middlesex from London.

## HEN AND CHICKENS, St Paul's Road, N1

A superb Victorian corner pub with a flourishing theatre above the bars that puts on both serious and comedy shows. The hen and chickens motif runs around the parapet. There are seats for 60 people, which came from the old Brighton Pier. Throughout the country several pubs are named the Hen and Chickens. It was a 17th-century expression for the Pleiades, a group of stars in the constellation Taurus. By the 19th century it was used to describe a children's game. In tavern slang a 'hen' was a large pewter drinking pot and a 'chicken' a smaller one.

## KING'S HEAD, Upper Street, N1

This is London's oldest pub theatre, and the till still uses pounds, shillings and pence. There is live music every night, except at Christmas, and there is singing around the piano. It is a Victorian pub with no juke box or fruit machines. The bar is a three-sided wooden counter on bare wooden boards and stage spotlights illuminate the customers while a fringe curtain decorates the top of the bar. The back-room theatre has been everything from a boxing ring to a pool hall. There has been a pub on the site for 500 years. The theatre was founded in the mid-1970s and has the usual theatre seats although some are at tables.

## LANDOR, Landor Road, SW9

The two faces of the theatre, tragedy and farce, are painted on the outside of this Victorian corner pub. Inside canoes hang from the ceiling and there is a

cabinet of pool trophies. There is a handsome bar and bare boards. Although only a few years old, the Landor Theatre has achieved notable successes. Above the pub, with a box office at the foot of the stairs, it seats between 40 and 50 with a wide programme from various theatre groups.

## LATCHMERE, Battersea Park Road, SW11

This is a vast Victorian corner pub with very high ceilings, ornate mouldings and dark oak furniture. There is a long bar and leather couches by the open fireplace. There are decorative lampshades to admire and even fresh flowers on the bar and tables. It is a good-sized theatre for a pub with 80 seats and was originally founded in 1982. The programme focusses on the future, with new writers, directors and up-and-coming comedians.

## LION AND UNICORN, Gaisford Street, NW5

This heraldic device refers to James I, Charles I and William and Mary. There have been stories about unicorns since 400 BC and they are mentioned several times in the Bible, where they were probably wild ox. The beast of the myth is white with the body of a horse and the tail of a lion, with a single horn. This Victorian corner  pub is noted in north London for its pub theatre. Outside is a fine tree covering a courtyard.

## OLD RED LION, St John Street, EC1

This is the most popular pub name and there are about 600 of them across the country. The red lion was the coat of arms of John of Gaunt, the power behind the thrones of Edward III and Richard II and patron of Geoffrey Chaucer. The Old Red Lion theatre is one of the oldest and best loved in London and was created in 1979. It became a noted pioneer of new talent in drama. The year that the V-sign of disrespect appeared, 1415, this pub first opened. The V-sign started at Agincourt when the French said they would cut off the pulling fingers of the longbowmen during one encounter. At the end of the day the English archers raised their two fingers in defiance – and the rest is history. Legend has it that Thomas Paine penned *The Rights of Man* here; but this is disputed by the White Hart at Lewes in Sussex, where he worked as a revenue man.

## O'NEILLS, Shepherd's Bush Green, W12

This is one of the most famous pub theatres and it started in 1972 when it was called the Bush. It has a fine reputation for its focus on new plays, and several playwrights have seen their work first performed here. Shepherd's Bush is an ancient piece of common land that got its name because shepherds used it on their way to Smithfield Market. It was first recorded in 1635. In the 1750s there was a public gallows at the eastern end of the ground. In the early 19th century no gentleman would venture over Shepherd's Bush without a pistol to protect himself.

## OXFORD ARMS, Camden High Street, NW1

Set in the middle of a market street, this is a bright, airy Victorian pub with some period pieces left. The Etcetera Theatre is housed in one of the smaller pub theatres and is accessed by narrow stairs at the rear of the bar. There are six rows of seats facing the stage and playgoers have often crashed into the actors as they come on and off stage. Occasionally two different plays are performed in an evening and they cover a wide range of theatre.

## PRINCE ALBERT, Pembridge Road, W11

This is a fine west London pub named after Prince Albert (1819–1861), who married his cousin Queen Victoria in 1840 and became Prince Consort in 1857. The Gate Theatre has its home above the pub and tends to focus on actors and acting rather than other parts of theatrical production. It has been here since 1979 and sets are minimal with flexible seating.

## ROSEMARY BRANCH, Shepperton Road, N1

There has been a pub here since 1783 and the rosemary branch was used for

decorations, especially at weddings and funerals. It symbolises both fidelity and remembrance. The pub, opened the same year as Newgate Prison and the death of Capability Brown, once had great tea gardens and was renowned as a music hall. Charlie Chaplin once played there. It is a large Victorian corner building with high ceilings, decorated pillars and a motley collection of tables and chairs. Large stuffed fish hang over the bar and local artists exhibit their work here. This includes a large statue of a naked man incongruously wearing a tie.

## ST CHRISTOPHER INN, Greenwich High Road, SE10

Pubs and inns were originally built for travellers and this is no exception. A large pub outside Greenwich station, it now caters for travellers from all over the world. Once called the Prince of Orange, the St Christopher is now part of an hotel chain. It is only a 15-minute journey from central London to this pub and theatre. The inn is near the Maritime Museum, the Naval College and the *Cutty Sark*, and is noted for innovative and unusual plays.

## TABARD, Chiswick, W4

The tabard was a short-sleeved surcoat decorated with the coat of arms of a knight and worn over the armour to show his identity. It is often associated with pilgrim pubs. The tabard was first used in Palestine to keep the heat off the knights' armour. Chaucer and his pilgrims set off for Canterbury from another Tabard pub in south-east London, which burnt down in 1676. This Tabard is a well-known pub with a renowned theatre. It has been haunted since the late 19th century by an elderly woman. Often she is seen sitting at a

St Christopher Inn,
Greenwich High Road.

table in the bar dressed all in black. She appears to be whistling but those who have seen her say no sound comes from her.

## THREE HORSESHOES, Heath Street, NW3

This is a wonderful Victorian pub with the Pentameter Theatre above the bars. Several pubs are named the Three Horse-shoes and the name refers to a horse on its way to a blacksmith's shop near the pub, when it would only have three shoes. It is also in the heraldry of the Worshipful Company of Farriers (1673) and the Ferrers family, earls of Derby. Their family name comes from a French place-name from the Norman Conquest. This area was known as Hemstede by 969 and Hamestede by 1086 and meant homestead.

## WHITE BEAR, Kennington Park Road, SE11

Set back off the road is this vast Victorian pub with a four-sided central bar and high-backed wooden stools. The pub name goes back to Henry III, who had his own white bear at the Tower of London. He kept it to put into the Thames to catch fish as a spectacle for visiting ambassadors. The white bear was adopted by Anne, consort of Richard III, as her personal emblem, and it is the heraldic device of the earls of Kent. A ship named the *White Bear* was part of Drake's squadron at Cadiz in 1587. By day it is a normal pub for locals and business people. In the evening it is taken over by playgoers. The theatre started 20 years ago and has since achieved success with awards as Best Fringe Venue.

# *Chapter 2*
# BOAT RACE PUBS

The first Putney to Mortlake boat race between Oxford and Cambridge was held in 1845 over 4.5 miles. It is the most famous of Varsity Matches and one of the most popular televised sporting events in the UK. This wooden bridge replaced the old ferry in the reign of George II in the mid-1750s.

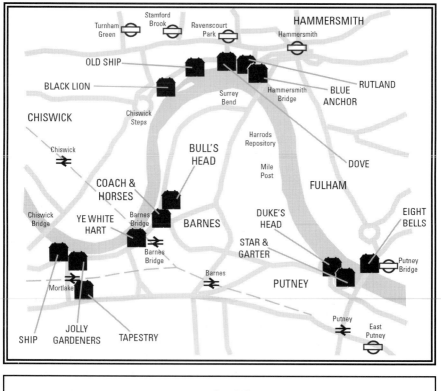

HAMMERSMITH

Turnham Green
Stamford Brook
Ravenscourt Park
Hammersmith

OLD SHIP

BLACK LION

CHISWICK

Chiswick Steps

Surrey Bend

Hammersmith Bridge

BLUE ANCHOR

RUTLAND

Chiswick

Harrods Repository

BULL'S HEAD

Mile Post

DOVE

COACH & HORSES

FULHAM

Chiswick Bridge

YE WHITE HART

Barnes Bridge

BARNES

DUKE'S HEAD

EIGHT BELLS

Barnes Bridge

STAR & GARTER

Barnes

PUTNEY

Putney Bridge

Mortlake

SHIP

JOLLY GARDENERS

TAPESTRY

Putney

East Putney

## North side

### EIGHT BELLS, Fulham High Street, SW6

The pub dates from the 17th century and is the oldest pub in Fulham. First licensed in 1629, it was known as the Blue Anchor, then the Anchor, Anchor and Eight Bells and the Eight Bells by 1754, the same year as the foundation of the Royal Society of Arts. Eight bells is the usual

number of bells in a peal and marks the end of a navy watch. The pub has wooden settle seats along the walls and many pictures of ships and the River Thames and an interesting old clock. It is a listed building.

## BLUE ANCHOR, Lower Mall, W6

On the river, this is a popular place on boat race day. The Anchor is the fourth

most common name for a pub. It was popular with landlords who had been to sea, and was an easily recognised sign to attract other seafarers. There is a secondary meaning as well, from St Paul: 'We have this as a sure and steadfast anchor, a hope' that relates to Christian belief. Many pubs had close connections with pilgrims and monasteries. This inn has rowing memorabilia and candles on the tables. The composer Gustav Holst lived across the river at Barnes and he composed the *Hammersmith Suite* here.

## RUTLAND, Lower Mall, W6

Just a few yards upriver from the Blue Anchor is the Rutland, providing grandstand views of the race. It is named after the smallest county in the country, which lost its status in 1974 in the carve-up of administrative areas, but has now been restored. There is usually jazz and blues here every Friday night. Hammersmith is first recorded as Hamersmythe in 1294, as a place with a smithy or forge.

## DOVE, Upper Mall, W6

The dove is the most sacred of birds and the Christian symbol for the Holy Spirit. The Dove is a 17th-century pub and boasts the world's smallest bar: 4ft 2in by 7ft 10in. They once squashed 20 people in here. The words for *Rule Britannia* were written here by Scottish poet James Thomson. Prince Augustus, son of George III, bought a smoking box here. (Aristocrats often had their own saloons in inns where they would smoke pipes and cigars.) Next door is a former home of William Morris, and Ernest Hemingway, A.P. Herbert and Graham Greene used the pub. The area has always attracted the wealthy and one of the first notable people to frequent it was Catherine of

Braganza, wife of Charles II. The king would also repair here to dally with Nell Gwynne. The pub featured in *The Water Gypsies* by A.P. Herbert as the Pigeon. Fullers' Brewery has owned it since 1796, when it was known as the Dove Coffee House.

## OLD SHIP, Upper Mall, W6

One of only four pubs in the census of 1722, this is the oldest pub in Hammersmith. Rebuilt in the mid-19th century it was moved westwards but retained some of the earlier features and is now a listed building. The area is no longer the industrial landscape it was in the 19th century, when there were mills, factories and sail makers for the shipping trade, as well as an old

brewery that was taken over by Fullers in 1923. On boat race day they set up a large TV screen. There is an upstairs room but it is first in, best placed.

## BLACK LION, Hammersmith, W6

At this inn close to the riverside a ghost was seen by a rat catcher and others in 1803. Before this it was seen by a pregnant woman. It chased her, gathered her up in its arms and she died of fright two days later. A local man was out one night when an excise officer, Francis Smith, looking for the ghost, saw something, fired and shot the nocturnal pedestrian dead. The victim was a builder called Thomas Millwood. At the inquest at the Black Lion the coroner said it was wilful murder and Smith was committed to the Old Bailey. There he was convicted of murdering Millwood, but afterwards pardoned. In the Long Room, a small child in Victorian clothing has been seen to skip around and is described as pretty, about eight years old and dressed like Alice in

Wonderland. The black lion was the heraldic device of Owain Glyndwr, a Welsh chieftain, and his father, Madoc ap Meredith. Outside the pub is an area to view the racers as they come to Chiswick Eyot, where the willow trees were cut back to provide fishing baskets for local trade. It was built on the site of a piggery under a centuries-old chestnut tree.

## South side

### STAR AND GARTER, Lower Richmond Road, SW15

At the start of the boat race the Star and Garter is the best place to watch the off. The top function room has the best vantage point, but if you arrive after 11am you don't stand a chance of seeing the race. The star and garter refers to the Most Noble Order of the Garter, the highest order of chivalry, created by Edward III in 1348. In 1750 there were three pubs on this site, the Star and Garter, Eight Bells and the Red Lion, which were all absorbed into this building under the Star and Garter name.

### DUKE'S HEAD, Lower Richmond Road, SW15

Upriver is the Duke's Head, with huge bay windows overlooking the river and

Star and Garter, Lower
Richmond Road.

a large lounge with a grand fireplace and mantelpiece. It is a popular name for a pub, and many Duke's Heads were named after whichever duke was the hero of the day. When it was built in the early 1800s it was not built for locals, but for Londoners on a day out in the country – Putney was a small village until the 1880s. There have been other pubs on this site and this was rebuilt in 1864. The three bars are Victorian design with etched and embossed glass, mirrors and carved mahogany fittings with deep comfortable armchairs.

## BULL'S HEAD, Lonsdale Road, SW13

This is the first home of modern jazz in Britain, with bands playing in a back room used for radio and TV broadcasting. Known as the Sign of the Rayne Deer in 1672 it became the King's Head until 1735 when it was run by the Ash

family. It was later rebuilt as the Bull's Head. John Waring, a Queen's Messenger and property owner, had the present building erected in 1845. Opposite was a trading wharf and the pub was a busy coaching inn. There was once a skittle alley here. With a large central bar it is choked to the gunwales on boat race day. From the retaining wall on the other side of the road there is a fine view as the boats come round the bend. The name of the village of Barnes was first recorded as Berne in the Domesday Book of 1086 and meant a place by a barn.

## COACH AND HORSES, High Street, SW13

An old coaching inn, painted white with a floodlit boules pitch, the Coach and Horses is a one-room pub with a three-sided bar. It is decorated with coaching paraphernalia, leaded and etched windows, fancy iron work, old bottles, wooden beams and rough plaster walls. There is an enormous wood-burning fireplace and a large seating area outside. The rear window from the courtyard is particularly attractive. It is a few yards from the river front and the lavatories are in the old stables. In October 1776 Barnes Churchwardens ran up a bill for eight pence for beer here, and in 1895 it became the headquaters of the Barnes Cycling Club. Customers include two living poets.

## YE WHITE HART, The Terrace, SW13

The oldest pub in Barnes, it was built in 1662 as the King's Arms and became Ye White Hart in the mid-1700s. It is a popular name dating from the reign of

Richard II. The hart, a male deer, was better known to people in those days, and made an attractive pub sign. Rebuilt 100 years ago, it has an imposing frontage onto the main road, part of the Tudor layout of local roads. Originally this was a large square, white building with a slate roof and portico. Several inquests were held here in the 1800s and long-time manager Stewart Sell tells of poltergeist activity in the cellars. One barmaid came up terrified out of her wits about something she saw and would never go down there again.

Overlooking the river is a long veranda, very popular on boat race day. There is a large central bar and rowing memorabilia of oars and a sculling boat fixed to the ceiling. The building has a touch of the 19th-century hotel about it, with tall columns and theatrical drapes. The ballroom was used for old time dancing and as a recording studio.

## JOLLY GARDENERS, Lower Richmond Road, SW14

On route for hundreds of spectators of the boat race is the Jolly Gardeners on Ship Lane. The first mention of it is in 1720, when it was referred to as the Three Tuns. It became the Jolly Gardeners when there was a rapid expansion in the number of commercial gardens in the area, which fed central London. The produce was transported by barge and boat. In the 18th century the pub was a billet for soldiers. In 1802 the landlord, Stephen Stilwell, was hanged for murdering his wife and she is said to be the resident ghost. Rebuilt in 1922, it has one large bar as well as music and function rooms. Opposite is the Tapestry, formerly the Jolly Milkman, a unique pub name. It is named after the world-famous Mortlake Tapestries, made by Flemish weavers from the early 1600s and now valuable collectibles.

## SHIP, Thames Bank, SW14

It is only a few yards to the finish from this 300-year-old pub and there are vantage points through windows overlooking the river. The Ship was once known as the Hart's Horn or the Hartshorns and took most of its trade from the nearby draw dock or wharfe. In Elizabethan times there was an underwater causeway to cross at low tide to Chiswick. Early in the 1600s it was known as the Blue Anchor and there was a nearby pub, the Maidenhead. It has a wood-panelled interior with nautical prints. Outside are seats and umbrella-covered tables for eating and drinking.

# *Chapter 3*
# THE BRITISH MUSEUM
# AND HOLBORN

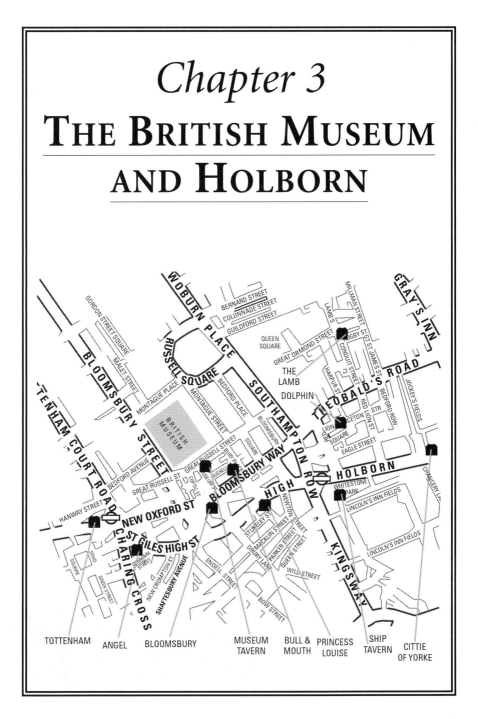

TOTTENHAM   ANGEL   BLOOMSBURY          MUSEUM      BULL &   PRINCESS      SHIP        CITTIE
                                        TAVERN      MOUTH    LOUISE        TAVERN      OF YORKE

## ANGEL, St Giles High Street, WC2

This is a three-bar pub with theatre posters in the smallest bar. The elegant central bar has cream and gilt stucco on the ceiling and a history of the pub on the wall. There has been an inn here for centuries and when it was called the Bowl, prisoners stopped here for their last beer before being hanged at Tyburn. One of them, a saddler called Bawtry, dispensed with this favour and went on to be hanged. Minutes later a pardon arrived, but the executioner had already done his duty. Now Bawtry haunts the pub. Public executions were finally banned in 1868. Once there were public hangings every six weeks, with up to 15 criminals being dispatched at each time. After the hanging there were fights to get the body between the Surgeon General's anatomy school and those who wanted parts of the body for good luck or to fend off disease. One murderer, William Duell, was found to be alive when they were about to dissect him two hours after execution. He was sent to Newgate and later transported to the colonies.

## BLOOMSBURY, West Central Street, WC1

Built in 1895 during the Gothic folly period, this pub became another home to the Bloomsbury set in the early 1900s and was the last 'wine only' house in

London. With an impressive exterior and leaded lights it has old beer barrels over the bar, shelf drinking with high stools and a tiled fireplace and partitions. It takes its name from Blemondisberi, the manor of William Blemond, who acquired the land in the 13th century. There are blue plaques in the area to some who drank here, including Vanessa Bell, Duncan Grant, Dora Carrington, biographer Lytton Strachey and novelist Virginia Woolf.

## BULL AND MOUTH, Bloomsbury Way, WC1

Near the British Museum, this corner pub is named after a battle won by Henry VIII in 1544, a corruption of Boulogne Mouth, France. Pubs called the Bull and Gate also commemorate this battle, as does the Bull and Bush, bush being a corruption of the French *bouche*, meaning mouth. A Victorian pub, it was the Bull and Mouth until 1982 when it the name was changed to the Falkland Arms for a short period, but it then reverted. Traditionally the name 'bull' is an ancient one for pubs and sometimes refers to a Papal Bull, the leaden seal attached to the Pope's edicts from the Latin, a *bulla*. A bull was also connected to the Royal Navy: it was a small keg, while to 'bull the cask' was to pour water into an empty rum cask and wait for the spirits to soak out.

## CITTIE OF YORKE, High Holborn, WC1

This is one of the treasures of London, with a huge vaulted ceiling in a

baronial sized hall and the longest bar in the capital. The Cittie is from a long line of inns that have stood here since 1430 but the earliest remaining sections now date from the mid-1600s. Today it is a fantasy of Gothic architecture with galleries, great windows and large wine tubs from a century ago. There is a huge Victorian clock on the outside. This design was part of a backlash by pub designers against the marble and glass gin palaces in high fashion then. They believed in drawing inspiration from earlier periods and used half-timbered gables, bottle-glass windows and black wood beams that were artificially warped and known as 'mock antique'. On the right-hand side there are wooden booths where members of the legal profession and others with dark secrets can talk in private. One bar is heated by a triangular-shaped coal stove dating from the early 1800s.

## DOLPHIN, Red Lion Street, WC2

When this pub was bombed by a Zeppelin air ship during World War One, three people were killed and many others seriously injured. In the explosion the pub was flattened but the pub clock remained intact. When it was rebuilt the clock was hung in the new bar. The hands have remained stuck at the time of the bombing, 10.40pm. Now, after the pub has closed, this stopped clock emits a long and low whistling sound that chills the blood of all who hear it. Gradually it quietens down and then the noise stops.

## LAMB, Lamb's Conduit Street, WC1

Built in 1729, the pub has Victorian 'snob' windows. The word 'snob' comes from a registration system at Eton College where pupils without rank were registered as *sine nobilitas* (without nobility), shortened to SN.OB. There is a polyphon, an forerunner of the modern jukebox, which can be played to collect money for charity. The Lamb of the pub name comes from William Lamb, a Gentleman of the Chapel Royal of King Henry VIII and a brother of the Clothworkers' Company. A water conduit was built in 1498 and Lamb improved it in 1577 at his own expense, spending £1,500. The water came through lead pipes and he gave the poor 120 pails to carry water. In 1667 the conduit was rebuilt by Sir Christopher Wren. The area was open fields then and the Lamb was, in its time, second home to the Bloomsbury set.

## MUSEUM TAVERN, Great Russell Street, WC1

Karl Marx used this pub when studying in London. It is opposite the British Museum and named after it. Up to the 1750s, when the museum was built, it was an alehouse called the Dog and Duck. This was because of duck hunting in the surrounding swamps. Redesigned by William Finch Hill in 1855, most

of what is in the pub now dates from this period, although the Victorian partitions have been removed. There is a half moon bar decorated with pre-war promotional mirrors. A tale is told of a visitor to the museum many years ago who asked where Karl Marx sat when using the study room. He was told, 'Oh, you mean the political theorist, Dr Marx. He left suddenly and has not been heard of since.'

## PRINCESS LOUISE, High Holborn, WC1

A gem of a pub, this establishment was named after Louise, the fourth daughter of Queen Victoria. She married the Duke of Argyll and died in 1939 aged 91. Designed by architect Arthur Chitty, it has tiles by Simpsons, glasswork by R. Morris and Sons and joinery by leading exponents of the art. The men's lavatory is of such special quality that it has its own protection order. Built in 1872, the pub is a listed building. It is unique in having a publican's office behind the bar for supervision. There is a U-shaped bar with a splendid period clock. Outside are vast wooden casks advertising their wares.

## QUEEN'S LARDER, Queen Square, WC1

George III was taken to a house near here by Dr Willis when he was unwell. Queen Charlotte kept his special food in a cellar at this corner alehouse. It then became known as the Queen's Larder. Larder is an old word for where food was kept fresh in a cool place before the days of refrigeration. The inn sign shows the Queen of Hearts hiding away her jam tarts, spied upon by the Knave. The first reference to this building as a pub was in a will dated 1718. It is set in an area of hospitals and foundling homes and Robert Louis Stevenson said of the area 'It seems to have been set aside for the humanities of life and the alleviation of all hard destinies.'

## SHIP TAVERN, Gate Street, WC2

During the 16th century Roman Catholics used this town pub for illegal masses. While the services were going on, men and boys were posted around

the area on the lookout for soldiers who would arrest and imprison them without trial if caught. There are still several priest holes where priests would hide until danger had passed. One of these priests still haunts the Ship and is noted for hiding articles and returning them several days later. Famous visitors to the pub have included Smeaton, who built the first Eddystone Lighthouse, and in 1786 it became a centre of Freemasonry.

## SWAN, Cosmo Place, WC1

No great distance from Great Ormond Street Hospital for Sick Children is the Swan. It is a street corner pub with wood panelling and stripped pine floorboards. There has been an inn on this spot since the 14th century and the sign of the swan was favoured by Edward III and Henry VIII as part of their heraldic design. The swan is never heard to sing but just before it dies it makes its swan song, which has come to mean one's last performance.

## YE OLDE MITRE, Ely Court, EC1

Bishop Kirby built a palace here in 1290 that became, in the 14th century, the

town residence of the Bishops of Ely, Cambridgeshire. The inn was built in the grounds and guarded at the gates by top-hatted beadles. Shakespeare set a scene from *Richard II* here, where John of Gaunt makes the famous 'sceptred isle' speech to his brother Edmund Plantagenet. In 1642 Ely Place became a prison and later a hospital for soldiers and sailors in the Civil Wars. The first Mitre was built in 1546 to house palace servants. In the bar there is part of a cherry tree trunk around which Elizabeth I danced when it was outside the present building. She allegedly visited it on several occasions during a love affair with Sir Christopher Hatton. The pub was carefully rebuilt in 1772 as an exact copy of the earlier pub, and the building is said to be haunted by a female ghost in 16th-century dress. Outside is an iron bar across the middle of the passage entrance to prevent horse riders getting through.

# *Chapter 4*
# COVENT GARDEN

COVENT Garden is of Saxon origin and was once a trading post known as Lundenwic. It was later a Convent Garden belonging to Westminster Abbey. In the 16th century the land was taken by Henry VIII and given to John Russell, Earl of Bedford. In 1627 he built the piazza that exists today. Drury Lane, named after the Hundred of Drury, was once lined with 107 pleasure houses, and a reverend in charge of moral issues said that the work done to reclaim this new Sodom would have paid for the force to conquer the Spanish West Indies. The first illicit gin outlet started here. Captain Dudley Bradstreet invented Old Tom: a carved wooden cat set into a wall from whence came one pennyworth of gin through the cat's paw. The Bow Street Runners were the first detective force, set up by Henry Fielding, magistrate, but were later named 'Peelers' under the command of Sir Robert Peel. All Victorian police stations had blue lamps outside except one: Bow Street. Queen Victoria passed it on her way to the opera and said that the lamp reminded her of the blue room in which her husband had died. So it had to have a white lamp.

## COACH AND HORSES, Wellington Street, WC2

One of the finest gems is to be found just off Drury Lane, in the street named after the Iron Duke. It is one of the last unspoiled mid-Victorian pubs and has a magnificent floral display. Part of the inside décor consists of theatre posters, but there are also designs with a curious golfing theme. For the whisky enthusiast there are 80 different varieties available.

## KEMBLE'S HEAD, Bow Street, WC2

John Phillip Kemble (1757–1823) was the most famous actor of his time, especially in tragic roles. He became a theatre manager in 1788 after being overshadowed by his sister, actress Sarah Siddons. This is a pleasant Victorian corner pub in Covent Garden with its history on an outside plaque.

## MARQUIS OF ANGLESEA, Bow Street, WC2

There have been licensed premises here since 1663, when it was known as Edward Miles' Coffee House. Opposite at 1, Bow Street, the Wills Coffee House known as Wits was made fashionable by Dryden, Pope and Macauley, and it was mentioned in Fielding's novel, *Tom Jones*. The surrounding area was lively and known for low life and brothels. This is a corner pub once used by traders from Covent Garden fruit market. It is named after the Marquis of Anglesey (sometimes Anglesea), who lost his leg at Waterloo in 1815 and kept it pickled for many years until it could be buried with the rest of him.

## OPERA TAVERN, Catherine Street, WC2

This really is a Phantom of the Opera pub, and was designed by Jonathon Treacher in 1879. It is used by singers from the Theatre Royal. Nearby is an

alleyway used by Charles II for assignations with Nell Gwynne. It is decorated with wooden panelling, etched mirrors and photographs of actors and singers who have appeared on the stage. The actor Richard Baddeley, who died here in 1794, haunts it. Over the years a rich actorial voice has been heard declaiming, and he has been seen in a long, dark cloak. Baddeley first appeared in 1761 and was a huge success in low comedy, making a fortune. When he died he left property to fund a home for 'decayed actors' and £3 a year for wine and cake in the Green Room at the Theatre Royal on Twelfth Night.

## PRINCE OF WALES, Drury Lane, WC2

The pub was established in 1852 by Henry Wells in a former potato warehouse and named after Queen Victoria's son, who became Edward VII. Drury Lane was a mediaeval route originally called the Via de Aldwych and renamed Drury Lane in 1500 after a barrister, Sir Robert Drury. It became of bad repute when two original plague sufferers died here – French sailors who had sailed from Holland. Mary 'Perdita' Robinson, model for Gainsborough and mistress of the Prince of Wales, lived nearby in 1774.

## WHITE HART, Drury Lane, WC2

There is evidence to suggest that this was an inn in 1216, making it the oldest in the capital. That was the year after Magna Carta and the year King John died. John Richardson's *Covent Garden* describes the pub as being there by 1570. However, it may be that this White Hart is confused with another, as E. Beresford Chancellor says in his *The Romance of Lincoln's Inn Fields and its Neighbourhood* 'the Aldwych Cross at the top of Drury Lane practically adjoined the White Hart, a tavern of great antiquity which existed until the 18th century when it was cleared by an act of George III.' If the pub really does date from 1216 it is the oldest in London by a good 150 years. Nowadays, the pub is 'cool'. It has a long, narrow bar with a marble bar top, comfortable armchairs and low tables. It is often given over to jazz. There is a light Art Nouveau touch in the chandeliers and wooden wall screen and triangular seats on iron bases stand with footrests.

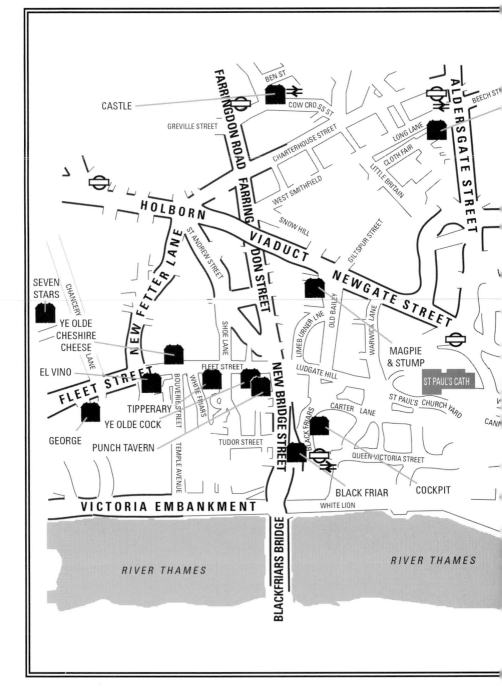

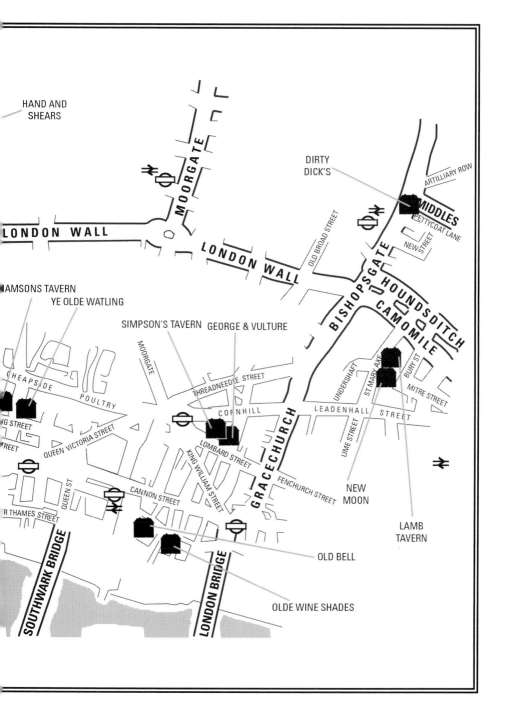

HAND AND
SHEARS

DIRTY
DICK'S

ARTILLIARY ROW

MOORGATE

MIDDLES

PETTYCOAT LANE

NEW STREET

LONDON WALL

LONDON WALL

OLD BROAD STREET

BISHOPSGATE

HOUNDSDITCH

CAMOMILE

AMSONS TAVERN

YE OLDE WATLING

SIMPSON'S TAVERN    GEORGE & VULTURE

MOORGATE

UNDERSHAFT

ST MARY AXE

BURY ST

MITRE STREET

CHEAPSIDE

POULTRY

THREADNEEDLE STREET

CORNHILL

LEADENHALL    STREET

LIME STREET

IG STREET

REET

QUEEN VICTORIA STREET

LOMBARD STREET

KING WILLIAM STREET

GRACECHURCH

FENCHURCH STREET

NEW
MOON

QUEEN ST

CANNON STREET

R THAMES STREET

SOUTHWARK BRIDGE

LONDON BRIDGE

OLD BELL

OLDE WINE SHADES

LAMB
TAVERN

41

Previous page: map features pubs that
appear in Chapter 5, Clerkenwell,
Chapter 13, St Paul's and Fleet Street,
and Chapter 16, The City and East
London.

# *Chapter 5*
# CLERKENWELL

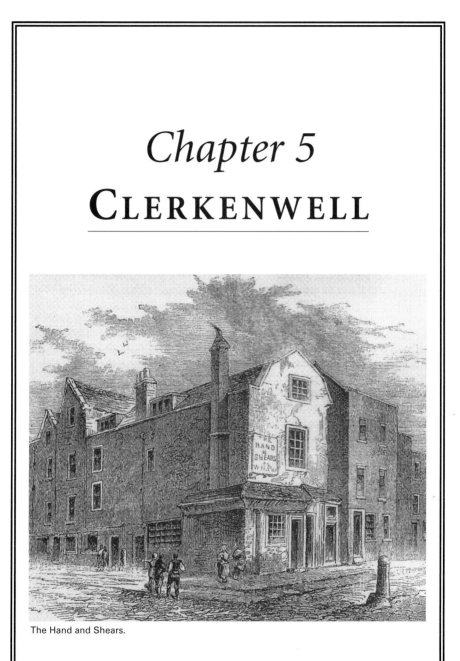

The Hand and Shears.

## ARTILLERY ARMS, Bunhill Row, EC1

Named after the Honourable Artillery Company (HAC), which had barracks nearby, this pub has been here since 1702 and was rebuilt in 1860. On the ground floor is a central island bar with cigarette card collections and old photographs. In an upstairs room are a marble mantelpiece and aquatints and paintings of the history of the HAC. This began as a guild of archers in 1537 and they maintain that they are the oldest and most senior regiment of the British Army. Bunhill Fields Cemetery is opposite, where John Bunyan, William Blake and Daniel Defoe are buried. Defoe was buried in 1731 but the tombstone was lost until 1940 and found as part of a fence at Southampton. Following the plague of 1665 the poet John Milton retired to this road, where he later died.

## CASTLE, Cowcross Street, EC1

The Castle is the only pub in London to have been licensed as a pawnbroker. George IV lost money gambling at a cockfight and, wearing a long cloak and

large hat to disguise his features, borrowed £1 against his watch from the landlord. Later a court official recovered it and the pawnbroking licence was granted. In one of the three bars hangs the sign of the three golden balls, although there is no pawnbroking today. It has bare wood floors with red walls and a large painting of George IV at the cockfight. He was a keen boxing fan and at his coronation Tom Cribb, champion of England, guarded the entrance to Westminster Hall.

## CROWN TAVERN, Clerkenwell Green, EC1

This inn was built on the site of an old nunnery and nun-like wraiths have appeared in the bars to the consternation of staff and customers. It was next to the London home of Oliver Cromwell and was used by cattle drovers coming in to central London from the north. Once there were tunnels to the local House of Detention. Russian revolutionary Lenin lived here when he was a student at the Karl Marx library. There is a main bar with smaller rooms running off and etched glass panes and decorative mirrors. Once known as the Crown and Apollo Concert Hall, there is a copy of an original poster of top acts.

## DIRTY DICK'S, Bishopsgate, EC2

This well-known watering hole was named after a wealthy shopkeeper, Nathaniel Bentley, in the late 18th century. He was averse to cleansing himself and was known as Dirty Dick. He had, in fact, been quite a dandy, but when his fiancée died, just before their wedding, he closed up the dining room at his home where the wedding breakfast was to have been held. The premises then went into decay, and were found half a century later. This is the basis for the famous character of Miss Havisham in Charles Dickens's *Great Expectations*. A landlord bought up the contents and put them on display and called it Dirty Dick's. In 1870 the place was rebuilt, with all the contents put back, but by 1985 the idea palled and everything was moved out, although the name remains. Now Dirty Dick's has bare floorboards, exposed brickwork and oak and glass screens.

## HAND AND SHEARS, Middle Street, EC1

A fine old tavern known locally as the Fist and Clippers. It has stood here for over 400 years and was built on the site of a former inn, an alehouse from 1123. The name comes from the cloth merchants at Bartholomew Fair who set

up stall in the 12th century. In the 16th century on 24 August, St Bartholomew's Day, the Mayor came out of the Hand and Shears to pronounce the market open and cut the first piece of cloth to be sold with a pair of tailor's shears. From this practice comes the custom of cutting a piece of tape or ribbon on special occasions. In an upstairs room was the court of Pieds Poudre (dusty feet), convened to hear complaints against local traders who sold short measure. If found guilty they were put in the stocks or whipped. The Bartholomew Fair ended in 1855. The history of the pub is displayed on a wall and they used to serve condemned prisoners their last pint on the way to the gallows. There are four bars served from a central island but one snug is so small it holds only eight customers.

Jerusalem Tavern,
Britton Street.

## JERUSALEM TAVERN, Britton Street, EC1

This is curiously named after the Knights Templar who protected Christian pilgrims going to Jerusalem. The order was suppressed for heresy in the early 14th century. At one time this tiny gem of a pub was a coffee house and is still fronted by a bowed window dating back 200 years. There are bare boards, an open fire and tiled pictures of the four seasons on the wall, and *Country Life* magazines are provided. It has high-backed settle seats without padding and huge brass candlesticks lit at night. Inside is a plaque of a dark bearded man. Is this Heraclius the Hospitaller, who offered Henry II the keys to David's Town, the Holy Sepulchre and the Kingdom of Jerusalem if he would lead a crusade? The pub was once a town house, built in 1720 when the area included watch and clock makers. West of here Ikey Solomons ran his vicious gangs of child thieves in the 1800s. He was the inspiration for the character of Fagin in Dickens's *Oliver Twist*. It was also this area that had the first gay pubs, known as 'Mollies', for working-class homosexuals. One of the most infamous in the 1700s was Mother Clap's Molly House, where she rented out dresses to men and hired rent boys.

## SEKFORDE ARMS, Sekforde Street, EC1

The pub is named after Thomas Sekforde, lawyer and Master of the Rolls and patron of Saxton the cartographer. Saxton is described as the 'father of English cartography'. Sekforde, whose family were lords of a manor in Suffolk, commissioned him to survey the kingdom. Sekforde's mottoes and coat of arms appear on every map authorised by Elizabeth I. The first country atlas came out in 1589. Near to the pub there is a curious address: No.18 and a half, Sekforde Street. This was once the Finsbury Bank for Savings, where Charles Dickens had an account. The Sekforde Arms itself was built in 1835 and is a small, wedge-shaped building, with paintings on the wall including the arms of the Sekforde family.

## SUTTON ARMS, Carthusian Street, EC1

Now here is a ghost of some distinction, for he has flaming red hair and over the years has been nicknamed Charlie. One woman, combing her hair in front of a mirror, saw Charlie standing behind her with a huge grin on his face. Two women lunching in the bar were astounded when a red-headed man wearing

old-fashioned clothing suddenly appeared between them. He gave them his cheery grin and disappeared. Although there has been research into Charlie no one has any idea who he is or why he is there. The street is named after monks who came from France and built a monastery. Later Thomas Sutton, merchant and philanthropist, turned the monastery into a hospital for the poor. The pub is named after him.

## YE OLDE RED COW, Long Lane, EC1

Long Lane leads off Cloth Street, near the priory of St Bartholomew, which was founded in 1123 by Rahere, court jester to Henry I, who became a monk. Close to the Smithfield Market, Ye Olde Red Cow caters especially to the

market porters in the area and opens early in the morning. There is a painting of the tavern as it was in 1854 in the Guildhall Library. A previous landlord, Dick O'Shea, haunts the pub. Once there was an internal balcony and O'Shea sat in his rocking chair gazing down on his customers before he died. As this balcony no longer exists he often appears in the bar.

# *Chapter 6*
# BUCKINGHAM PALACE

Buckingham Palace is the first home of the monarchy. When George IV came to the throne he wanted Buckingham House, as it was then known, rebuilt. Instead it was redesigned by John Nash and cost over a million pounds. Queen Victoria, crowned in 1837, became the first British monarch to live there.

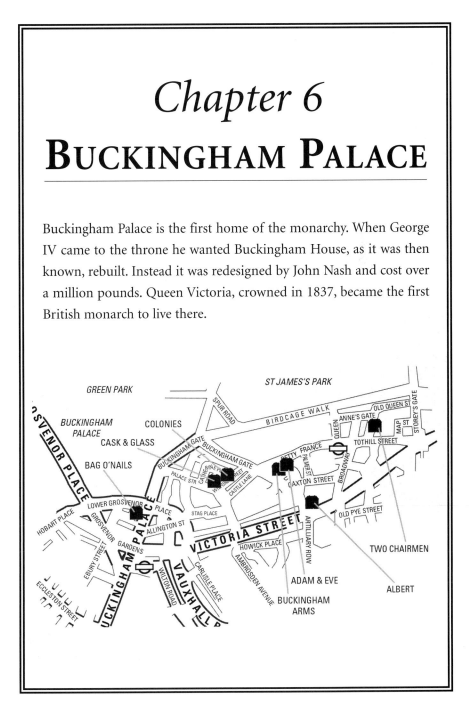

## ADAM AND EVE, Petty France, SW1

One of the last gas-lit pubs in the capital, this is the third to stand here since 1649. The present pub dates from 1661, the same year the Board of Trade was founded and hand-struck postage stamps were first used in this country. The sign, Adam and Eve, was that of the Fruiterers' Company. Petty France was named after French wool merchants who lived there in the 17th century. One resident, Cornelius Van Dun, Yeoman of the Guard of Henry VIII, Edward VI, Queen Mary and Queen Elizabeth I, built almshouses nearby for 20 poor women to dwell in rent-free. John Milton, Latin secretary to Cromwell, wrote most of *Paradise Lost* while living in Petty France. There used to be an Adam and Eve at Paradise in Gloucestershire, which has now sadly gone.

## ALBERT, Victoria Street, SW1

Often used by Chelsea Pensioners, this is a large Victorian pub that was

originally called the Blue Coat Boy in 1831 and was renamed the Albert after the Prince Consort when it was rebuilt in 1864, the same year the Albert Memorial was started. It is one of London's most attractive pubs, with cut-glass windows, a splendid wooden bar topped by a large clock and original gas lights outside still working. The staircase is the central feature here: it is on a grand scale, with portraits of British Prime Ministers from Salisbury to Tony Blair hanging above it. Margaret Thatcher unveiled her own portrait.

## ANTELOPE, Eaton Terrace, SW1

An unspoiled pub in a back street, the Antelope was built in 1827 for the servants of the local aristocracy and gentry. It has splendid wood panelling and an island bar with side alcoves. Once this was a swamp area frequented by robbers and highwaymen. Then Thomas Cubitt constructed London's finest houses, which became Belgravia. When it was divided into separate bars each was used by different levels of rank of servants. The antelope is on the heraldic signs of Henry IV, V and VI and those of the dukes of Bedford and Gloucester. Ships of the Royal Navy have been called *Antelope* since the 16th century and one was sunk in 1982 in the Falklands.

## BAG O' NAILS, Buckingham Palace Road, SW1

This pub is the closest to Buckingham Palace and, when built in 1775, it was called the Devil and Bag O' Nails. It is a street corner pub with a wooden panelled interior. In 1838 it was rebuilt, a year after Queen Victoria came to the throne. Now it is a listed building with Scottish plaids on the wall. The name was originally that of the ironmonger when tradesmen displayed their trade sign and the ironmonger's was a bag of nails, although some maintain it is from the Bacchanals, a Roman festival dedicated to Bacchus, god of wine.

## BUCKINGHAM ARMS, Petty France, SW1

This is an elegant pub with a long curved bar and a side corridor drinking area that must be the narrowest bar in the world. The pub has leaded windows and is a listed building. Off the main bar there is a dining room and there are etched mirrors behind the bar. It was first licensed in 1780 as the Black Horse, the same year that General Cornwallis defeated the Americans in the Carolina Campaign and the first Derby was run. It was renamed the Buckingham when rebuilt in 1901.

## CARDINAL, Francis Street, SW1

For over 150 years this pub stood as the Windsor Castle and was renamed the Cardinal because it is near the home of the Roman Catholic Church of Britain, Westminster Cathedral. It has maintained its Victorian design of panelled wood walls, a well-designed fireplace, cut-glass windows and a mahogany bar with elaborate lamp holders. Apart from lavish mirrors there are portraits of cardinals over the years and one appears on the inn sign. In AD 975 this area was known as Westmynster, or West Monastery.

## CASK AND GLASS, Palace Street, SW1

Not far from Scotland Yard, this pub was saved at the last hour when due for demolition and is one of the smallest pubs in the capital. Used by MPs, actors from the Palace Theatre and staff at Buckingham Palace it is a Shepherd Neame pub, the oldest brewery in England, and until recently sold beer only in half pints. There is old panelling and the room is decorated with prints of MPs and Lords, and model aircraft. The L-shaped bar is decorated at ceiling level with plates. The Cask was first licensed for 'beer only' in 1862 when it was the Duke of Cambridge.

## COLONIES, Wilfred Street, SW1

First licensed in 1785 as the Pineapple, the Colonies took a colonial theme 25 years ago and is split-level. When the pineapple was introduced to this country in the 17th century it was a huge novelty. Some pubs named this were near markets that sold the fruit. The pub is decorated with skins and trophies from the days when Britain had influence throughout the world. Pineapple is also the slang for a bomb or hand grenade and was an heraldic device of the kings of France.

## HORSE AND GROOM, Groom Place, SW1

First licensed over 150 years ago, this is a tiny mews pub with wood panelling. It is hidden away in the elbow of a cobbled yard with fine houses around it, and was given its name because of the number of grooms and stables nearby. It is on the western side of Buckingham Palace and was once a favourite drinking place of the Beatles.

# *Chapter 7*
# BELGRAVIA AND
# KENSINGTON

**CHURCHILL ARMS,** Kensington Church Street, W8

The pub is named after Winston Leonard Spencer Churchill (1874–1965), Britain's leader during World War Two and twice Prime Minister. Apart from his political career he wrote history books, biographies and memoirs, the best known being the *History of the English Speaking People* and a biography of John Churchill, Duke of Marlborough. In 1953 he was awarded the Nobel Prize for Literature. The pub is charming and atmospheric with a collection of 1,600 butterflies, 100 chamber pots, brasses and copper ornaments and pictures of past Prime Ministers and American Presidents from Washington to Nixon. The passageway to the lavatory is called 'Chamber Lane'.

**FOX AND HOUNDS,**
Passmore Street, SW1

This is a popular name for a pub and not just in hunting country. It was the last 'beer only' house in London and has a collection of Toby jugs and Spy prints on the wall. There were many 'beer only' houses in London because the Victorians believed that spirits were bad for the working classes. Built in 1860 at the end of a terrace of cottages built for artisans, the Fox and Hounds has a number of small, narrow bars. There is a list of previous monarchs and books in glass-fronted cases. Locals include Chelsea Pensioners and the cast from the Royal Court Theatre.

## GRENADIER, Wilton Row, SW1

Set in a mews, the pub is haunted by the ghost of a young Grenadier officer caught cheating at cards. He was beaten to a pulp and thrown downstairs to his death. Reports have been made of shapes and chills around the pub. Once a brewery inspector, a former CID man, was burned on the wrist as though by a cigarette, but no one was there. A man who took his own life by electrocuting himself in a bathroom also haunts the pub. Once the mess for the Duke of Wellington's officers, the bar has sabres, daggers and bugles hanging from the ceiling, plum-coloured walls, wooden floors and a pewter-topped bar that is 200 years old. Outside is a sentry box and the duke's stone horse-mounting block. A notice outside claims that the pub will only serve people arriving on foot, by taxicab or by cycle. Medium Trixie Allingham said that a most serious quarrel once took place here and that there was a ghost in the cellar. Originally called the Guardsman, the pub is most haunted in September, when the cheating officer died.

## NAG'S HEAD, Kinnerton Street, SW1

One of the last free houses, the pub has the lowest beer counter in the capital at just over two feet high. The bar staff stand on a lowered floor behind it. Built in 1780, when there were many stables in the area and horses running about on the Grosvenor Estate, it was partially rebuilt in 1833, the same year

the Factory Act forbade employment of children under nine and gave freedom to British colonial slaves. In a cul-de-sac there is a narrow, wood-floored bar, and a stone-flagged bar with a cast-iron fireplace and model aircraft. Usually the Nag's Head referred to an inn that hired horses. The Victorian beer engines to draw the beer from the barrels were made for the Great Exhibition and the pumps have original Chelsea Pottery handles. There are Victorian entertainment machines, fortune telling and caricatures of pub regulars and actors including James Mason. It has the largest collection of unusual items I have come across in a London pub.

## PLUMBER'S ARMS,
### Elizabeth Street, SW1

Since 1974, when Lord Lucan disappeared, this pub has drawn people from across the world. It was here that Veronica, Countess Lucan, fled after the attack on her and the murder of her nanny. Nothing has been seen of Lord Lucan since, despite reported sightings worldwide. Many books have been written about him and the police files are still open. Built in 1821, the present frontage went up in 1852. It is a small plush bar with an upstairs restaurant. The sign of the Plumbers' Company Guild, granted in 1588, is above the door. Now in a most salubrious area, there were two bars and a 'bottle and jug' where local wives would collect beer for their husbands.

## STAR TAVERN, Belgrave Mews, SW1

This four-storey building in a quiet, cobbled mews was built for the local servant population in 1848, the same year that Karl Marx's *Communist Manifesto* was published. The mews were used to house grooms and horsemen but are now expensive town houses. The pub gained a raffish reputation at one time, with a mixture of villains and celebrities happily drinking together. (Until film star Elizabeth Taylor was told to shift her 'fat bum' off a bar stool.) The story of this and other incidents are pinned up in framed clippings. With an open bar it has two fireplaces in the largest room, scrubbed pine tables and a fortune-telling machine for charity. The star is a religious sign referring to the Star of Bethlehem or the Virgin Mary, one of whose titles is Star of the Sea. Since 1643 a 16-point star has appeared on the arms of the Worshipful Company of Innkeepers.

# *Chapter 8*
# CHELSEA

This area was known as Celcythin in AD 789, meaning a landing place for chalk or limestone. By 1086 the name had become Chelchede, which finally gave rise to the modern name of Chelsea.

World's End.

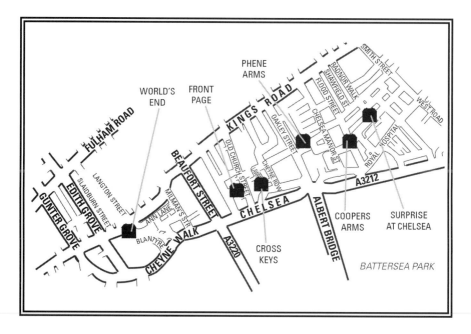

## ADMIRAL CODRINGTON, Mossop Street, SW3

Sir Edward Codrington (1770–1851) was at the Battle of Trafalgar and was captain of the 98-gun *Orion*. He was commander-in-chief of a joint British,

French and Russian fleet that defeated the Turkish and Egyptian navies at Navarino Bay. Known as the Admiral Cod, the pub was built in a market gardening area near a street called Green Lettuce Lane. Divided into three parts with bowed and mullioned windows on the first floor, it has bare floorboards and a covered rear garden for al fresco drinking. It is decorated with polished brass and copper, pewter mugs and Toby jugs. Famous 'Sloane Ranger' customers included Lady Diana Spencer.

## ANGLESEA ARMS, Selwood Terrace, SW7

The pub is named after the Marquis of Anglesea, Henry William Paget (1768–1840), a general at Waterloo. He lost a leg in a skirmish when shot by a

cannon ball. Paget looked down and said, 'By God, sir. I think I have lost my leg.' To which the Iron Duke (Wellington) replied, 'By God sir, I think you have.' Paget had the leg pickled on the battlefield and it was buried with the rest of him 40 years later. Charles Dickens knew the Anglesea Arms as he lodged at No.11 Selwood Terrace when courting Catherine Hogarth, his wife. The Great Train Robbery was planned here. There is a large open bar with half partitions to divide areas with button-back padded leather seats, and the pub is decorated with ornate mirrors and prints and original 'snob' windows.

## AUSTRALIAN, Milner Street, SW3

This mid-19th-century pub used to be next door to the Prince's Cricket Ground, Lennox Gardens, where England played Australia in the first home match in 1878. It was then named the Australian. There is a vast creeper covering the frontage, and inside are two bars and a brass-topped counter. Cricket memorabilia includes oddly shaped bats, old prints and photographs of Australian cricketers over the years.

## COOPER'S ARMS, Flood Street, SW3

The old village of Chelsea was built around the church of St Luke's and Flood Street was named after Luke Thomas Flood. The Cooper's Arms is first mentioned in the Post Office Directory of 1846, but it is known to have been there much longer. Entering this pub you are greeted with a stuffed bear, a hanging moose and a deer's head over the door to the lavatories. The time is shown on a huge station clock. (Next door is St Loo Avenue; did Thomas Crapper, the manufacturer of the modern lavatory, live there?)

## CROSS KEYS, Lawrence Street, SW3

The ghost of a landlord murdered here in 1911 still makes his presence felt occasionally. Built as modern Gothic with a bit of modern tat, there is an

engraved mirror with a huge lion peering out from an embossed centre, and a plastic monk with his habit heaved up leaning over the fire. The cross keys is common in Christian heraldry and there are many such pub names. First licensed in the 17th century, it has stone flag flooring with a galleried function room.

## FRONT PAGE, Old Church Street, SW3

Built over 300 years ago as the Black Lion and rebuilt in 1892, the Front Page has an L-shaped bar with high ceilings, old panelling, bare boards, wooden furniture and an open fire. When it was the Black Horse two women who had enlisted in the army drank there. They were Christina Davis, who served with the Royal Irish Enniskillen Regiment, and Hannah Snell of Guise's Regiment of Foot and, later, the marines. Snell received a pension for life from the Chelsea Hospital, the home of the Chelsea Pensioners. Old Church Street is

the oldest in Chelsea and the church nearby dates from the eighth century. When Dean Swift lived here he described the haymaking nymphs as 'pitiful drabs' compared with country girls. Nearby King's Road was a country lane through fields for market gardeners and farmers. In 1660 it became the direct route between St James's Palace and Hampton Court, and it was a private road for royalty with day tickets issued for commoners until 1830.

## PHENE ARMS, Phene Street, SW3

Famous for planting trees throughout London, Dr John Samuel Phene lived

nearby in Victorian times. His programme was supported by Queen Victoria, which led to the idea being copied in many cities both here and abroad. Trees Dr Phene planted himself still exist and the pub is surrounded by a fine array of honeysuckle that shades the beer garden. The street was named after Dr Phene, followed by the Phene Arms. He lived in a weird building called Gingerbread Castle, a monstrosity that was pulled down in 1920. It is sad that the Phene has lost some of its original Victorian features. It is still a cosy pub with an island bar and many paintings by local artists. Famous customers have included George Best the footballer.

## SURPRISE, Christchurch Terrace, SW3

Down the back streets of Chelsea, this pub has not changed much over many years. Considering the area it is an ordinary down-to-earth pub with a dartboard. Surrounding the horseshoe-shaped bars are plain benches, wooden walls and a bare oak wood floor. Built in 1853, it took its name from two Royal

Navy ships called the *Surprise*, one which took Charles II from Brighton to France after the Battle of Worcester and another which took Napoleon's body back to France in 1821.

## WELLESLEY ARMS, Sydney Street, SW3

Built in 1823 when St Luke's Church was being erected, there is said to be an underground passageway between the pub and the church so clergy could visit. Charles Dickens married Catherine Hogarth in the church in 1836. Named after the Duke of Wellington, Arthur Wellesley (1769–1852), who laid the first stone of the church, the pub sign portrays the duke who became a British national hero after defeating Napoleon at Waterloo in 1815. Later he became a fairly reactionary Prime Minister and served as Home Secretary in 1834. Born in Ireland he was once asked how he felt about his Irishness and he replied, 'Jesus was born in a stable but he didn't think he was a horse.' For years there have been stories of a ghost here who makes his own breakfast.

## WORLD'S END, King's Road, SW10

In the days of Charles II this was a tea garden and pub. The name has been in

use since the 17th century and there is another famous World's End at Knaresborough, Yorkshire. Congreve refers to this pub in *Love for Love* and Pepys indulged a lady there. He wrote 'We ate and drank at the World's End where we had good things'. In the nearby Cremorne Gardens a balloon ascent was made to a height of two miles by Mr Hampton, who descended by parachute. This balloon flying became quite an event, with comedians singing songs while many feet high and lady astronauts taking off in classical costume.

# *Chapter 9*
# CHISWICK

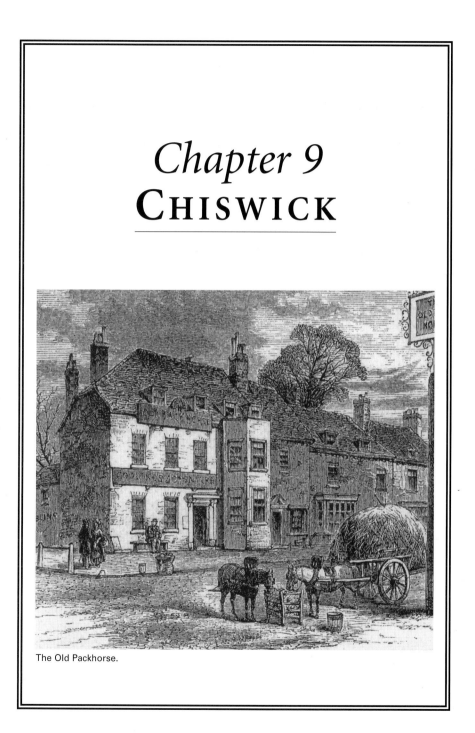

The Old Packhorse.

## BELL AND CROWN, Strand-on-the-Green, W4

A superb inn, it has a conservatory furnished with cane chairs overlooking the river. The first mention of Chiswick is as Ceswican in AD 1000, and the name meant 'the farm where cheese is made'. The Bell and Crown pub name derives

from loyalty to the throne, because bells would be rung from churches on special royal occasions. Many bells, when cast, had inscriptions put on them that were later transferred to inn signs, such as 'Fear God' and 'Honour the King'. The bar is kept warm by a log fire.

## BULL'S HEAD, Strand-on-the-Green, W4

An inn has stood on this riverside site for 400 years. Oliver Cromwell dined here when visiting his sister nearby and was told Royalists were on their way to arrest him. He fled via an under-river tunnel to an island (now Oliver's Ait)

Bull's Head, Strand-on-the-Green.

and then took a boat to the other side. Cromwell was almost the first victim of a machine-gun attack. In 1657 Miles Syndercombe hatched a plan with others in this pub to use an early version of the gun to assassinate Cromwell as he travelled from Hampton Court through Shepherds Bush. He was betrayed by one of the gang and, after their dastardly plot was revealed, was tried but died before he could be executed. Over the years the pub has grown and changed and now there is a fascinating collection of rooms differing in size and character. There are low ceilings with bare floorboards and light comes through small leaded windows.

## CITY BARGE, Chiswick, W4

On a fine riverside walk is the City Barge. Over 500 years old, it was damaged during World War Two and has since been partially rebuilt. Originally the Navigator's Arms, it had (until some evil-doer made off with it) a charter from Elizabeth I. In 1619 it changed its name to the Bohemia Head after the Elector

Palatine Frederick V married Elizabeth, daughter of James I. It remained the Bohemia Head until 1788, then took its present name because the Lord Mayor of London's ceremonial barge berthed here for the winter. The pub occasionally floods from the river so there are no cellars. It has one of the few remaining Parliamentary clocks, which were left open-faced to avoid a clock tax. Part of the film *Help*, starring the Beatles, was filmed here. Nearby is St Nicholas's church, where William Hogarth, James Whistler and two of Oliver Cromwell's daughters are buried.

## CROWN AND ANCHOR, Chiswick High Road, W4
This is the name of a pub often chosen by retired naval chief petty officers, and

derives from their arm badge. The tune for the American national anthem, *Star-Spangled Banner,* originated at the Crown and Anchor, the Strand, in 1790. It was an original English song and the pub was used by the Anacreontic Society for singing and orchestral pieces. The music *To Anacreon in Heaven* was penned by John Stafford Smith. The society took its name from a Greek poet who lived 2,500 years ago who wrote in praise of wine and song. It stands opposite Turnham Green where in 1642 there was a battle between Royalists and Roundheads. For many years the area was notorious for highwaymen and footpads. Built in 1825, the Crown and Anchor was one of 21 pubs in the High Road, most of which are long gone.

## OLD PACKHORSE, Chiswick High Road, W4

Before the canals and railways horses were used for heavy transport of corn and wool and this road was a main entry into London. The packhorse men used these inns at regular intervals and many were named for them. This is a fine example of opulent late Victorian style, with great pillars, exterior tiling and etched glass. Inside are ceiling-high mirrors with a glass emblem of the Old Packhorse.

# *Chapter 10*
# SOHO

CENTURIES ago this was hunting land named after the hunting cry 'So' (see) and 'ho' (after him). Tally ho translates from Norman French as 'there he goes'. In the 18th and early 19th century it was the art centre of London with the foundation of the Royal Academy. There were shops for clockmakers, boot and shoemakers, toymakers and gold-smiths. The finest tapestries of the day were created in Dean Street and are now known as Soho tapestries, and have become great collectibles.

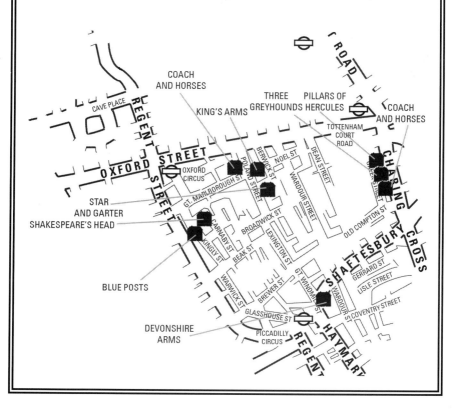

## ARCHERY TAVERN, Bathurst Street, W2

When George III celebrated his quarter century on the throne in 1785, this inn was first licensed. It was also the year of the Battles of Quebec and Warburg when the French were defeated by British and Prussian troops. Built on Archway Mews, there are still working stables at the pub. There was considerable interest in archery nearby and the Royal Toxophilite Society practised at nearby archery butts. The society is named after a book, *Toxophilus*, published in 1545 by

Roger Ascham, and the name means 'lover of the bow'. The pub has a bucolic charm, with timber fittings and wooden half-panelled walls. The main bar has potted plants to give a country air and there is bow and arrow artwork on the walls.

## BLUE POSTS, Kingly Street, W1

The pub is tiny for central London and is named after the four corners of the hunting grounds of Soho. Called King Street until 1906 the '-ly' was added to avoid confusion with other King Streets. Some of the windows are bowed, single panes of glass. There were coloured posts throughout England to indicate houses before numbering started in the 18th century. As such, Blue Posts would have been a description of the house rather than the name of it. There is a great deal of wood in the pub, with barrel tables and shelves of books.

## COACH AND HORSES, Greek Street, W1

A well-known Soho pub, named Norman's after a previous landlord, Norman Balon, said to be the rudest landlord in London. Once frequented by *Private*

*Eye* staff and playwright Jeffrey Barnard, there are three drinking areas with Heath cartoons and a portrait of the landlord. It dates from 1847 when the novels *Jane Eyre, Wuthering Heights* and *Agnes Grey* were published by the Brontë sisters and chloroform was first used as an anaesthetic.

## COACH AND HORSES, Great Marlborough Street, W1

In the same year that Dick Turpin was hanged, 1739, this large-fronted tavern was opened. It was later rebuilt as a Victorian-style corner pub with a wooden fascia and some reproduction prints on the wall. Upstairs is the Laughing Horse Comedy Club.

## DE HEMS, Macclesfield Street, WC1

In a tiny street off China Town, this is a fascinating pub. There has been an inn here since 1688, when it was called the Horse and Dolphin. In that year William of Orange ascended the English throne after James II. It became a meeting place for Dutch immigrants in the early 1900s when Mr De Hem, a

retired merchant seaman, took over and created a whole Dutch atmosphere that became famous for beer and oysters. Once there were 300,000 shells decorating the walls but they were taken out in the 1950s for safety reasons. It maintains some Dutch history with pictures of windmills, Breughel prints and two Dutch football team shirts worn and signed by Dennis Bergkamp, the Arsenal player.

## DEVONSHIRE ARMS, Denman Street, W1

One of the few buildings in the West End to escape damage in World War Two, the Devonshire Arms opened in 1793, the same year £5 banknotes were issued and the first free settlers arrived in New South Wales. There was a coaching station opposite and passengers waited at this inn. The street was named after Dr Thomas Denman, who ran the local medical school. The pub has a very curious bar shaped like a triangle. Once gangland villains met here to make their wicked plans; now it is more likely to be the Greenwich Industrial History Society.

## DOG AND DUCK, Bateman Street, W1

A small pub with two bars. The ground floor has maintained its old character with ornate wood panelling, etched glass and mirrors, a marble fireplace and tiles with the dog and duck motif. It was rebuilt in 1891 but a pub of the same name has stood here since 1734 when Soho was hunting country; hence the name. There are tiled pictures throughout in the same manner as Victorian grocers, butchers and fishmongers. There is a tiny rear room heated by an open fire in winter. Famous customers have included Mozart, Rosetti, Constable, George Orwell and, more recently, Madonna and her husband, Guy Ritchie.

## FITZROY TAVERN, Charlotte Street, W1

This is the only pub known to have given its name to the district where it was located. Bohemian customers named the area around the pub Fitzrovia in the 1930s and it stuck. The customers over the years read like a litany and include politicians, artists, writers, philosophers, painters, prostitutes and spies. Augustus John, the artist, said that if you have not visited the Fitzroy, you have not visited London. Portraits of John adorn one wall. It is a large square room

with an island bar and small, cosy alcoves. Downstairs is a well-panelled and leather club room for artists and writers.

## GUINEA, Bruton Place, W1

There has been an inn here for 400 years, possibly since 1423, and it was first called the Guinea in 1755. Before that it was the Pound, after a cattle pound nearby. Once renamed the Guinea it was referred to, in merry jest, as Ye Olde One Pound One. The guinea was first struck as a coin in 1663 and was worth one pound, or 20 shillings. In 1717 it became tender worth 21 shillings. The original coin, made from gold from Guinea, West Africa, carried the picture of

an elephant. Journalists and lawyers were paid in guineas until the 1960s. Elizabeth II was born around the corner at 17, Bruton Street, in 1926. The Guinea catered to the servants and stable hands from the fashionable houses in Bruton Street and Berkeley Square.

## KING'S ARMS, Poland Street, W1
Over 200 years ago the Ancient Order of Druids was revived in a tavern that

stood on the same site as the King's Arms. This was 28 November 1781 but the pub dates back to 1728. That year marked the end of the war between Spain and England and the first public performance of John Gay's *Beggar's Opera*. The landlord is an honorary member of the Ancient Order of Druids.

## PILLARS OF HERCULES, Greek Street, W1

The Pillars is named after two rocks marking the entrance to the Mediterranean, the Rock of Gibraltar and Mount Hacho. In ancient legend it is said that they were once one rock, torn apart by Hercules to get to Cadiz.

Hercules, or Heracles, is the most popular hero of Greek and Roman legends. Part of the pub dates back to 1733 and Dickens refers to it in *A Tale of Two Cities*. One character, Dr Manette, gave his name to a street at the side of the pub. Some old décor survives; snob windows, a decorated plaster ceiling, hanging lamps and a bare wooden floor.

## SHAKESPEARE'S HEAD, Carnaby Street, W1
A fine pub named after playwright and poet William Shakespeare. Born at

Stratford-on-Avon he was married to Anne Hathaway and thought to have been a schoolteacher for some time. After arriving in London he became connected with the theatre and was the author of 37 plays and much poetry. He must be rotating in his crypt over this pub name, for in *Titus Andronicus* he talks of some men as 'ye alehouse painted signs' meaning they were not real men but copies of them. Built in 1735, the pub was originally owned by Thomas and John Shakespeare, distant relatives of the playwright. The inn sign is a reproduction of the portrait of

Shakespeare by Martin Droeshouts. A life-size bust looks down on the world-famous shopping precinct with one hand missing; this came off during a bombing raid in World War Two.

## STAR AND GARTER, Poland Street, W1

The name dates from 1348 when Edward III picked up a garter dropped by the Countess of Salisbury at a ball. Handing it to her he noticed courtiers sniggering and placed it on his own leg saying, 'Honi soit qui mal y pense' or 'Evil be to he who evil thinks'. This became the Most Noble Order of the Garter and is limited to the sovereign, members of the royal family and 25 knights. This small, old-fashioned pub, built in 1825, has wooden panelling with bare wooden boards. On a painted mirror is the Star and Garter insignia.

## THREE GREYHOUNDS, Greek Street, W1

Although this refers to greyhounds used as hunting dogs when Soho was open

country, it could refer to stagecoaches calling here as many were called 'greyhounds'. The hunting dog was known as a gazehound because it relied to a large extent on sight rather than scent. Nowadays greyhounds are seldom used for hunting except by poachers who cross them with collies to produce lurchers. The ancient name for greyhound racing was greycing. There has been an inn here for five centuries according to writing left on a wall by an artisan. The mock-Tudor front was added in 1920. The greyhound was the heraldic device of the dukes of Newcastle.

## TOTTENHAM, Oxford Street, W1

At one time there were 32 pubs in Oxford Street but now there is only one, the Tottenham. Built in 1790, it was refurbished 100 years later and called the Flying Horse. It is a lavish pub in the Victorian style with paintings, mirrors

and carvings all executed by master craftsmen of the day. There is a splendid glass dome and murals of naked nymphs on the ceiling. The area was once the Manor of Tothele, and is mentioned in the Domesday Book of 1086.

## TYBURN, Edgware Road, W2

Now a large glass-fronted pub, there have been Tyburn inns and taverns for over 300 years and this was previously the Marble Arch. It was near here that public executions took place from the 12th century to 1783. The permanent

gallows, the Tyburn Tree, provided popular entertainment. It gave rise to two expressions still used. 'One for the road' meant the last pint drunk by a felon before hanging and 'on the wagon' came from the guard who was left on the hanging wagon, and not allowed to drink, while other guards drank with the condemned man.

## YE GRAPES, Shepherd Market, W1

Shepherd Market is one of the villages of central London with small shops in narrow streets around this pub. Built in 1882, when the Ashes were instituted in cricket, it was infamous for prostitution. Now Ye Grapes shines like a moral beacon with dark painted walls, tiles and light-coloured bricks. There were many partitions but several fireplaces show how it was arranged with Victorian pieces including stuffed birds, animal horns, porcelain figurines, huntsmen's rifles and a long-case clock. Everywhere are carved bunches of

grapes. Edward Shepherd built Shepherd Market in 1735 on the site of an old fair. This was an annual event under charter from James II in 1688, but it closed down in 1708 because of bad behaviour.

# Chapter 11
# WHITEHALL, WESTMINSTER AND ST JAMES'S

## CLARENCE, Whitehall, SW1

There is a long bar here with gas lighting, exposed beams, a bare wooden floor and brickwork. It was once called the Duke of Clarence. This royal duke (1765–1837), third son of George III, became William IV. He served in the Royal Navy but was so bad at taking orders that he was never allowed to command a ship. Even so, he was promoted to Admiral of the Fleet in 1801. He took his seat in the House of Lords and was later known as the Sailor King.

He introduced the Royal Navy tradition of toasting the King sitting down because the ship's timbers were so low he kept banging his head. When Scotland Yard was nearby the Clarence was known as the 'copper's nark'.

## GOLDEN LION, King Street, SW1

This pub has been here for over three centuries. Many pubs are called the Golden Lion and it was the heraldry of King Henry II and the dukes of

Northumbria. Over 200 years ago a woman kicked the landlady to death and there have been reports she is still in residence and can be heard shouting. The pub features memorabilia from St James's Theatre that existed from 1835 to 1957. There are rich stone decorations from roof to pavement designed by architects Eedie and Meyers. Rebuilt over a century ago, there are ornate carved lions, bow fronts, leaded windows and a Theatre Bar. A blue plaque exists to Napoleon III, Emperor of France, who lived nearby in 1848.

## OLD SHADES, Whitehall, SW1

If the royal family were to have a local it would be this, as it is licensed by Buckingham Palace. It is a long, narrow pub that widens out at the rear and is designed in what was called Flemish-Gothic style in 1898. It is a listed building. There have been several older pubs on the site going back 400 years. A picture of the Queen hangs in the bar. Shades is an old fashioned word for shadows or ghosts. Perhaps there are long-forgotten stories of this pub being haunted.

## RED LION, Duke of York Street, SW1

An absolute gem of a pub, first licensed in 1688 and rebuilt in 1871, the Red Lion retains its original engraved glass, decorative mirrors, mahogany fittings, crystal chandeliers and an island bar of polished mahogany. Outside it is plain brick, with ornate ironwork with cascades of flower baskets. Once it took its customers from the servants of the grand houses around. During one renovation exact copies were made of ceilings and plasterworks. There were five bars, including a 'bottle and jug', but now there is just one. In the year it was built there is the first reference to Lloyds of London when Edward Lloyd set up his coffee house to deal in finance.

## RED LION, Parliament Street, SW1

On the corner of Parliament Street, this is an ornate pub with an impressive interior and original mahogany woodwork and cut-glass mirrors. If,

perchance, you see a number of people suddenly get up and rush out, leaving their drinks behind, you can bet they are MPs at the House of Commons who have heard the division bell ring. In the cellar bar there are NUM banners as a memento of when the pub was the unofficial HQ in the miners' strike of the early 1970s.

## RED LION, Crown Passage, SW1

A small pub in an alleyway off Pall Mall, the Red Lion is the second oldest licensed pub in the West End. Inside is a great deal of wood panelling and leaded windows. Crown Passage opens out at the side of Quebec House, built in 1673. Externally it is a black part-timber frontage with leaded light windows. Old gaslight brackets have electric fittings and narrow stairs lead to a dining room. On the last Saturday of January each year Cavaliers, dressed to the nines, parade here to lament the death of Charles I, executed in Whitehall on 30 January. Crown Passage is one of the most redolent of old London and is eight feet wide with shops on either side.

## SILVER CROSS, Whitehall, SW1

Near the Houses of Parliament, this pub has a unique name and a long narrow bar with a high vaulted ceiling. First licensed in 1674, it was granted a brothel licence by King Charles II for personal services rendered. It is Crown property and was originally licensed by the Board of the Green Cloth. (This was because the King's Steward and his board sat around a table covered with a green cloth. It started with Henry I and was abolished in 1849.) Cromwell's

house was on the other side of the road. A small girl wearing Tudor costume haunts it. She is a happy child who sings, giggles and skips around the house. Occasionally there has been the sound of a woman's voice calling out the name of a boy.

## TWO CHAIRMEN,
### Dartmouth Street, SW1

The pub is named after the men who carried sedan chairs around London. When introduced to this country in 1630 by Prince Charles (later Charles I) and the Duke of Buckingham on their return from Spain, the custom was widely decried as being brutal to the carriers. As people left fashionable addresses they would shout 'Chairo!' to call for a sedan, which eventually became 'cheerio', as a form of farewell. London sedan chairs were stationed at fixed points and one of the first of these was this pub. At one time there were hundreds of sedan chairs and it cost one shilling an hour for two men to carry a chair. The pub is 17th century with interesting murals on the walls.

## WESTMINSTER ARMS, Storey's Gate, SW1

Not far from the Houses of Parliament and Big Ben, the Westminster has been a well-known watering hole for politicians and journalists for many years. Every now and again the ghost of a small boy appears with burn marks on his face. He is dressed in 17th-century clothing and appears to be weeping. The legend is that he died in a fire at or near the pub, 350 years ago. It was called the Red Lion until 1969.

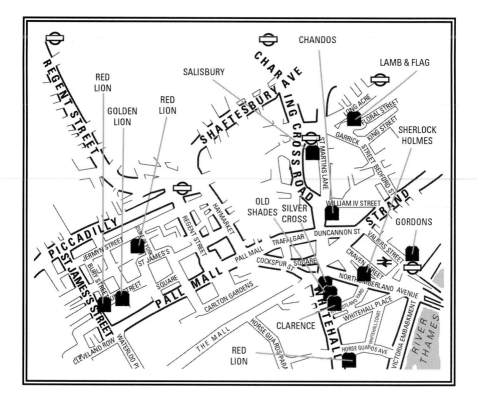

# *Chapter 12*
# THE STRAND AND
# TRAFALGAR SQUARE

**COAL HOLE,** The Strand, WC2

From mediaeval times coal was brought into London by barge and one entry point was Carting Lane, where the Coal Hole stands. An old alehouse, it was used by the coal carriers and merchants that gave rise to its name. It is in Savoy Buildings, designed by Thomas Collcutt and built of stone with leaded windows. Inside is a high ceiling and a gallery at the rear overlooking the main bar. Built on several earlier pubs in 1904 it is decorated in Art Deco style with a marble frieze of maidens picking grapes. Actor Richard Harris used to wander here when living at the Savoy. Upstairs is the Wolfe Room, named after the Shakespearean actor Edmund Kean's (or Keane's) club for errant husbands.

## CHANDOS, St Martin's Lane, WC2.

This was named after Lord Chandos, patron of the German composer Handel when he was working in London. Chandos's ancestor was a man who made a fortune as a continental raider during the Hundred Years War in the struggle to control France for dynastic ambitions and trading purposes. It has won many prizes for design that is basically late Victorian but redesigned with hand crafted good quality joinery and tile work. In the bar are bare boards with small booths and upstairs is an Opera Room. Highwayman Claude Duval was caught in the Hole in the Wall tavern close by while drunk.

## GEORGE TAVERN, Strand, WC2

Opened in 1723 as a coffee house, the George has its own fashionable ghosts. One has been there for many years and is called George after the pub. I like his style: he is a Cavalier with a beard and a plumed hat, who sits on beer barrels in the cellar watching people work with a world-weary smile. Also haunted by a judge in full regalia, the George is mock-mediaeval half-timbered and was a well-known coaching inn and staging post. The inn sign depicts George III but the pub is named after its original owner, George Simpkins.

## GORDON'S WINE BAR, Villiers Street, WC2

If you don't like this wine bar then there is something wrong with you.

Gordon's claims to be the oldest wine bar in the capital and was granted a licence to trade in wines by Edward III in 1364. It is a super bar near Charing Cross station and there have been many reports over the years of the haunting there. Some have said unseen eyes were watching them and others say they felt a tap on their shoulder and a voice in their ear as they stood against the bar. The furniture is eccentric, to say the least, with bare wooden chairs and candlelit tables; but the wines are superb. There is a narrow and steep staircase into the dark vaulted bar and antique prints and newspaper front pages covering main royal events.

## LAMB AND FLAG, Rose Street, WC2

Since the time of Queen Elizabeth I an inn has stood here and it is the oldest in Covent Garden. The name comes from the heraldic device of the Knights Templar, Merchant Tailors' Company and St John's College, Oxford. The lamb

is of great importance in the Christian faith, from St John: 'Behold the Lamb of God which taketh away the sins of the world.' Usually such signs portray a lamb with a banner wrapped around it. The pub was previously known as the Cooper's Arms, from the 16th-century Coopers' Company which built barrels and tubs in wood with staves and hoops. Once bare knuckle-fights took place upstairs with many guineas and property changing hands in bets. It was then nicknamed the Bucket of Blood. John Dryden, poet, was almost murdered outside by a violent gang on behalf of a mistress of Charles II in 1679.

## LYCEUM, Strand, WC2

The Lyceum was the gymnasium and grove beside the temple where Aristotle

and other philosophers taught their brands of philosophy in Ancient Greece. Although there may well be high-level discussion here, this pub was named after the Lyceum Ballroom that is now the Lyceum Theatre. There has been an inn here for 300 years but historical detail is somewhat vague. There are many nooks and crannies and partitioned booths.

## NELL GWYNNE TAVERN, Bull Inn Court, WC2

This city tavern looks as many did five centuries ago in a narrow alleyway off the Strand. On the site of a 16th-century pub called the Black Bull, the Nell Gwynne is named after the most famous courtesan of English history. The alley leading off to Maiden Lane is flagstoned, with lanterns. Nell Gwynne was the driving force behind founding Chelsea Hospital and lived at Bagnigge Wells House in King's Cross Road. Once her coach was surrounded in London by a mob that thought she was a French whore of Charles's. Nell stuck her head out and shouted, 'Good people, be civil: I am the Protestant whore.' Bagnigge Wells became a teahouse and carries the oldest advertisement in London, dated 1680, and a place for rusticating Londoners. 'The Cits to Bagnigge Wells repair, To swallow dust and call it air' (Anon). In 1760 a bust of 'Eleanor Gwynne, a favourite of Charles II' was found here by Dr Bevis. When Charles delayed in conferring an honour on their son she held the boy from an upper floor window at Lauderdale House saying, 'Unless you do

something for your son, here he goes'. Charles replied, 'Stop Nelly, save the Earl of Burford'. The boy was later duke of St Albans. On his deathbed Charles said, 'Don't let poor Nelly starve'. In 1897 the actor, William Ferris, was slain outside the tavern and he still haunts the pub. In the 19th century a large population of black people lived nearby who used this pub for their parties, which were called 'black hops' or 'black routs'.

## SALISBURY, St Martin's Lane, WC2

This famous inn was acquired from the Marquis of Salisbury in 1892 and named after him. Four times Prime Minister from 1885 to 1901, his portrait is on the inn sign. Built on the site of a former pub, the Coach and Horses, the Salisbury was rebuilt in 1898. It was then that the double 'S' was etched into

the windows. At the time there was a huge call for elaborately designed pubs and the Salisbury did not fail. There are large mirrors, cut and etched glassware and mahogany. Art Nouveau light fittings in bronze show nymphs with long stemmed flowers and light bowls at the centre. The graffiti is Chaucerian.

## SEVEN STARS, Carey Street, WC2

This is the street where debtors trembled in fear of their fate. Near the Royal Courts of Justice, the pub was built in 1602 as the Leg and Seven Stars, a corruption of League and Seven Stars. It was a year old when Elizabeth I died at Richmond. Seven stars was a religious symbol and the sign of the Worshipful Company of Innkeepers. The pub has a long, narrow bar decorated with caricatures of famous legal men and women over the years. A few yards away are two of the capital's older parish boundary markers. These are stones marking the dividing lines between St Clement Danes and St Dunstan in the west.

The street is named after Nicholas Carey, who lived in Fickett's Field, belonging to the Knights Templar. Dickens worked an apprenticeship at the nearby Old Buildings.

## SHERLOCK HOLMES, Northumberland Avenue, WC2

Dedicated to the famous detective and his creator, Sir Arthur Conan Doyle, the pub has a museum including the head of the Hound of the Baskervilles, a

violin, extracts from the novels and portraits of actors who have played the sleuth. Why is it not situated at 221b, Baker Street? Well, it was at the nearby Northumberland Hotel that Holmes first met Sir Henry Baskerville. For many years the pub was known as the Northumberland Arms. Following the Festival of Britain an exhibition toured North America and a tableau of Holmes's study was about to be ditched. It was bought by Whitbreads and put behind a glass screen upstairs in the pub, which was then renamed the Sherlock Holmes. There is an international Sherlock Holmes Society and some members will not accept that he was a fictional character who first appeared in 1891.

## YE OLDE WHITE HORSE, St Clement's Lane, WC2

A great find near the London School of Economics, up a tiny lane named after the church of nursery rhyme fame. The white horse was adopted by the aldermen of Wessex, vassals to the kings of Wessex, and is now the traditional emblem of Kent. A sign of a galloping white horse was the heraldry of the House of Hanover from 1714, on the accession of George I. It also figures in the heraldry of several guilds: Carmen and Coachmen, Farriers, Innkeepers, Saddlers and Wheelwrights. On the small side, this is a cosy red-painted pub with a raised seating area at the rear.

# *Chapter 13*
# ST PAUL'S AND
# FLEET STREET

Built by Sir Christopher Wren, the cathedral dominates Ludgate Hill and is near where London's oldest curfew gate stood on the hill. It is the highest point in the city and the western end is the site of the old Fleet River. A cathedral has stood here since the early 1300s. In 1665, during the Great Fire of London, it was burnt out.

## BELL, Bush Lane, EC4

One of the smallest pubs in the capital, parts of the Bell survived the Great Fire of London and that makes it one of the oldest pubs in London. It was named because a church bell near here sounded the alarm for the Great Fire. When the Thames was much wider, before it was embanked, this was a riverside pub. There are two small rooms with wooden beams, a tiled floor and a huge number of prints and newspaper clippings hang about the pub. It is a listed building and there is no music, jukebox or TV.

## BLACK FRIAR, Queen Victoria Street, EC4

The Black Friars were a Dominican order known by the colour of their robes, who had a monastery here in the 13th century. This was closed down during the Dissolution of the Monasteries in 1538. The area became wasteland and in

1596 the actor James Burbage bought the land and built Blackfriars Theatre. William Shakespeare bought into the enterprise and took a house in Ireland Yard. The first staging of *Henry VIII* took place on this very site. By reputation the monks were fond of their beer and I am reliably informed by an expert in these matters that their beer was far stronger than that brewed today. The Black Friar is unique in being wedge-shaped, in Art Nouveau style, with marble arches, mirrors and most attractive gold and coloured mosaics. There are bas relief bronze pieces of monks about their business on the outside. It was a favourite of the poet John Betjeman and the current building is over a century old.

## COCKPIT, St Andrew's Hill, EC4

As a reminder of what this 400-year-old pub once was, there is a viewing gallery looking down as though into a cockpit. Once it was a venue for cockfighting where fortunes were won and lost. In 1849, when cockfighting was made illegal, it was renamed the Three Castles, a reference to the arms of the Worshipful Company of Masons created in 1677. Part of the building was bought in 1616, just before he died, by Shakespeare as a safe house for Roman Catholics. Renamed the Cockpit in the 1970s, it has a single bar with red velvet walls decorated  by the cock bird, framed prints, foreign bank notes and hanging ale jugs.

## EL VINO, Fleet Street, EC4

Enter El Vino and turn your watch back over a century. Opened in 1879, it has seen few changes and has a lot of wood and worn leather seating. Old bottles and barrels abound and it is as comfortable as an old club. The side alley was known as Ram Alley in the 1700s and is now Hare Place, thought to be a corruption of Whore Place. It achieved an historical point over a quarter of a century ago when women demanded to be served at the bar, and they are now more than welcome. It was once a haunt of barristers and senior journalists, but the latter have left because of the demise of Fleet Street as the centre of newspapers.

## GEORGE AND VULTURE, St Michael's Alley, EC3

This is one of three inns in the alleyways opposite the Royal Exchange with a unique name. In 1666 there was a tavern here, the George. This inn was razed to the ground. A wine merchant who had a tethered live vulture as an

advertisement took on part of the pub but the overall landlord objected to a live bird outside, although he agreed to change the name to the George and Vulture provided that the creature was taken away. Scrooge, of Dickens's *A Christmas Carol*, had his offices nearby and Mr Pickwick dined here while awaiting his trial. A parish boundary passes through the building, and the boundary marks are on the wall above the bar. It is haunted by a woman in Victorian garb in the upper eating rooms and other parts of the building. She wears a long grey dress, a small bonnet and a weary look.

## JAMAICA WINE HOUSE, St Michael's Alley, EC3

Hidden away in the narrow alleys of the city, this splendid Victorian inn was built on others going back to the original coffee house of 1652. This was when traders in Jamaican rum and sugar frequented the place and it was named after them. That same year Bengal became a British settlement. According to a plaque outside the pub, 'Here stood the first London coffee house at the sign of Pasqua Rosee's Head 1652'. In the Great Fire of London it was destroyed and finally rebuilt as the present

one in 1862 when the first Lambeth Bridge in London opened.

## MAGPIE AND STUMP, Old Bailey, EC4

A centuries-old pub, now modernised, the Magpie and Stump is opposite the Central Criminal Court. A previous inn sign showed a bird sitting on a stump.

This was similar to a white falcon on a tree root, the arms of Ann Boleyn. Old Bailey was first established in 1539 and was part of Newgate Prison that replaced Tyburn. The Magpie was where condemned men had their last pint when hangings took place outside. The inn rented out rooms with a view for £10 a time, with wine and a 'hanging breakfast' of meat and pies. In 1868 when Michael Barrett, the last man to be publicly hanged in England was executed for trying to blow up Clerkenwell Jail, over 100,000 people gathered. In 1780 the pub was wrecked in the Gordon Riots and in 1807 it became a temporary hospital for 30 people who were crushed trying to get into the court for a famous trial.

## OLD BELL, Fleet Street, EC4

Once second home to Fleet Street journalists, this low-ceilinged inn, built in 1670, is off St Bride's Avenue. When church building was in progress masons and artisans, employed by such as Wren, were housed here. Then they were working on St Bride's church. This church was badly damaged during the Great Fire and rebuilt by Wren. The design of the church inspired the tiered wedding cake. Poet John Milton lived at St Bride's Passage and during the plague moved to Chalfont St Giles.

There were other pubs on the site prior to this called the Twelve Bells, the Swan (where Wynkyn de Worde, an assistant to William Caxton, had a room in 1500) and the Golden Ball. Inside it is a most comfortable pub with dark oak panelling and small separate nooks and triangular-shaped wooden stools.

## OLDE WINE SHADES, Martin Lane, EC4

This is another city tavern that survived the Great Fire of London, having been built in 1663. It was originally the home of a nobleman. Cannon Street,

nearby, was called Candlewick from the candle makers who lived there and was afterwards taken over by drapers. Martin Lane slopes down to the Thames and is 100 yards from the Monument. Charles Dickens drank here when it was known as Henderson Shades and there is an old smoking room with oil paintings and cartoons. In the cellars is a bricked-up passage-way that used to lead to the river and was used by smugglers. When the earth floor in the basement was relaid some old clay pipes and round-bottom bottles were found. The London Stone, a Roman

artifact to measure distances from London, is a round boulder set into the southern wall of nearby St Swithin's church. Now measurements are from Charing Cross. Strype described the Roman Stone as old and worn before the Fire of London and Shakespeare writes of it in *Henry VI*.

## PUNCH TAVERN, Fleet Street, EC4

Meetings of the editorial staff of *Punch* were held here for 150 years. The lobby is decorated with tiles and mirrors and the glass panels inside are etched with birds.

Opened in 1841, there are Punch and Judy puppets in display cases and paintings and framed copies of *Punch*. It was previously known as the Crown and Sugarloaf. In the 1800s sugar was sold in conical-shaped loaves, like an ice-cream cornet. The sugar loaf was the sign of grocers and innkeepers. The pub displays some early 19th-century clocks and Art Nouveau chandeliers.

## SIMPSON'S TAVERN, Ball Court, EC3

Simpson's is hidden away in mediaeval-sized alleys and is one of the last survivors of the London chop-houses of the 18th century. Once it was two

houses, which were converted into a tavern in 1757, the same year that Tennessee, US, was first settled. Alterations were made and it became a two-storey building and the bow windows came later. In 1808 it was owned by Tom Simpson and, on his death, the new owner opened the restaurant that exists now. The dining rooms have been left much as they were and tables are arranged within stalls as was the wont of such chop-houses.

There is even a Dickensian-style top-hat rack for the convenience of gentlemen.

## TIPPERARY, Fleet Street, EC4

This pub was built on the site of a 13th-century monastery on an island between the rivers Thames and Fleet. Part of the Fleet still passes underneath the pub, which was built in 1605 as the Boar's Head. That sign dates from the 14th century, and comes from the old Christmas custom of serving a boar's head with an apple or lemon in its mouth. It survived the Great Fire of London because it was built of brick and stone. In 1700 it was bought by S.G. Mooney of Dublin and became the first Irish pub. There was a clock built by

Thomas Tompion that was stolen and then replaced by a replica. In 1918, when printers who had used it came back from the war, it was renamed the Tipperary after the famous war song. The first floor is still called the Boar's Head.

## WILLIAMSON'S TAVERN, Groveland Court, EC4

Near St Paul's Cathedral this 18th-century tavern maintains that it has the oldest excise licence in the capital. It was built off an alley after the Great Fire of London in 1666. Like many city buildings it covers old Roman ruins and there are still some old tiles. Once the building was the residence of the Mayor of London and William III and Queen Mary entertained here. They donated the wrought-iron gates that still guard the inn. In 1739 Robert Williamson turned it into a tavern and there is a portrait of him in the bar. There are three bars and one contains an old stone said to mark the centre point of the City. At one time it was the home of Sir John Falstaff. Bare boards with ironwork lamps and a touch of Art Nouveau décor make it a place to treasure.

## YE OLDE CHESHIRE CHEESE, Fleet Street, EC4

Following the plague and fire of London, Ye Olde Cheshire Cheese was rebuilt in 1667. It is on Wine Office Court, where a guesthouse for the Carmelite Order in the 13th century once stood, and there is evidence of this in the cellars. It was built in 1538 and during the 18th century was a chop-house of good repute. It was then home to the 'hackney writers', men hired to rewrite copy at a penny a line; their name was later shortened to 'hacks'. Dr Johnson lived around the corner and was a well-known customer. There are several

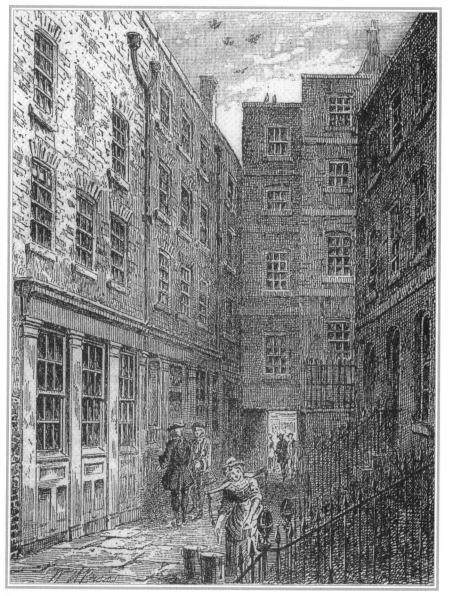

bars and dining rooms with passageways leading between them. The main oak table was used by Johnson, Charles Dickens, Oliver Goldsmith, Mark Twain, E.M. Forster, Alexander Pope and George Bernard Shaw. Dickens uses the pub in *A Tale of Two Cities* and it was a watering hole for journalists. Once there was a pub parrot, Polly, and on Armistice Night 1918 it imitated the sound of a champagne cork popping 400 times, then collapsed and died.

## YE OLDE COCK, Fleet Street, EC4

Another former home-from-home for journalists, this pub is haunted by Oliver Goldsmith, the Irish playwright. There is a fireplace reputed to have been carved by Grinling Gibbons, the world-famous wood carver, born in Rotterdam in 1648. He arrived in England in about 1670 and was promoted by a number of patrons including Charles II. Gibbons was also a favourite of the architect of the day, Sir Christopher Wren. There is a picture of Oliver Goldsmith on the first floor and because of this a woman was able to identify him in a terrifying haunting. She said she was working in the bar and suddenly before her very eyes appeared a grinning head at the back door. It was that of Goldsmith and since then others have reported seeing him with more of his body showing. Goldsmith is buried in the church of St Mary nearby. T.S. Elliott held editorial meetings here for the *Criterion* in the 1920s.

## YE OLDE WATLING, Watling Street, EC4.

After the Great Fire of London this pub was used to house workers building the nearby church of St Mary-le-Bow. It follows the custom of City pubs and the front bar has no tables or chairs and you drink standing up at a shelf around the wall. In the 14th century the bells of St Mary-le-Bow on Cheapside tolled the curfew at 9pm. It is built on the old Roman road, Watling Street, that ran from Reculver on the Kent coast through to North Wales. Watling is a corruption of the original name. Up to the mid-14th century it was known as Atheling Street, or street of the nobles, but by 1500 it had become Watheling Street, changing to Watling Street by the mid-1700s. At the time of the wild speculation that led to financial bubbles two wicked plots originated here. One entrepreneur sold the idea of square cannons with square projectiles to save on storage space, while another floated a proposition which had to be kept secret but requested gentlemen to put up £2 a share. The con artist concerned took over £2,000 in two days and was last seen boarding a boat for France.

# Chapter 14

# SOUTHWARK

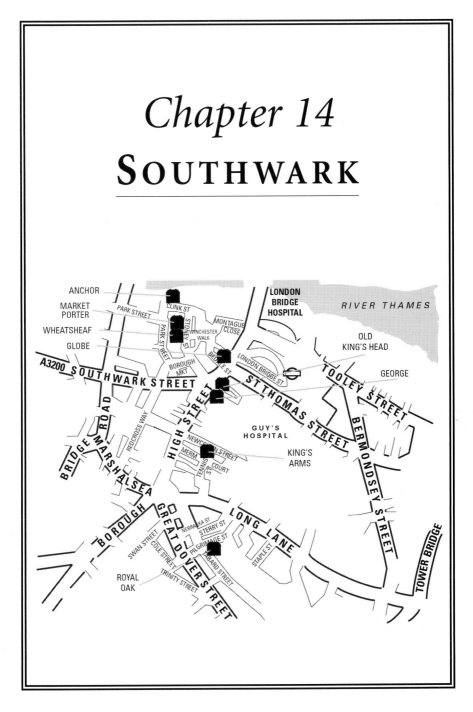

ANCHOR
MARKET PORTER
WHEATSHEAF
GLOBE

PARK STREET
CLINK ST
PARK STREET
STONEY ST
MONTAGUE CLOSE
WINCHESTER WALK
BEDALE ST
BOROUGH MKT
LONDON BRIDGE ST

LONDON BRIDGE HOSPITAL

RIVER THAMES

OLD KING'S HEAD
GEORGE

A3200 SOUTHWARK STREET

TOOLEY STREET

ST THOMAS STREET

BRIDGE ROAD
MARSHALSEA
REDCROSS WAY
HIGH STREET
NEWCOMEN STREET
MERM COURT
TENNIS ST

GUY'S HOSPITAL
KING'S ARMS

BERMONDSEY STREET

BOROUGH
GREAT DOVER STREET
SWAN STREET
COLE STREET
NEBRASKA ST
STERRY ST
PILGRIMAGE ST
TABARD STREET
STAPLE ST

LONG LANE

TOWER BRIDGE

ROYAL OAK
TRINITY STREET

## ANCHOR, Clink Street, SE1

One of the last remaining pubs of the Stews of London, the Anchor was built at the time of Elizabeth I. Samuel Pepys watched the Fire of London from here in 1666. There is a slave collar in a case behind the bar. The pub has several split-level bars, old beams, leather seating and quiet alcoves. The Anchor was close to the old bear garden, the Globe Theatre 200 yards away, and Clink Prison, next door. Clink is the old word for a prison, where men, women and children were locked up for many offences, including debt. Press gangs descended on pubs such as the Anchor to fill their ships with sailors. In one raid here they chose a man with a dog that attacked the press gang, one of whom slammed a door on it, cutting off the dog's tail. The man was dragged off to serve in Her Majesty's Navy and the dog escaped. Since then there have been sightings of the mutilated beast wandering around the pub and howling. One bar is named after Dr Johnson and there is a copy of his dictionary on display.

## ANGEL, Bermondsey Wall East, SE16

That hideous lawyer, Judge Jeffreys, still haunts this building from where he used to watch public hangings. Built in the 17th century on previous inns of the 15th century, it overlooks the Thames. Pepys, the diarist, knew it well. (He is said to have gone off to buy fruit from the local Cherry or Chalbate Springs Gardens but was really visiting a mistress, one Mrs Bagwell.) Once the monks of Bermondsey Abbey sold beer to travellers and local people. There were trap doors here used by river smugglers and Turner was inspired to paint the *Fighting Temeraire* after he saw it being towed to the breakers' yard from the Angel. The area was used by Dickens when Bill Sikes met his fate in *Oliver Twist*.

A royal manor house was built by Edward III on the site of the Angel and the King's Stairs was the landing point. Later it became a hospice for Bermondsey Priory. Captain Jones of the *Mayflower* used it to buy supplies, trade cargo and raise crews before the historic trip to North America in 1620. Captain Cook spent months at this inn preparing for his historic voyage. It was used as a pub in the *Long Good Friday* film. In AD 712 the area was known as Vermundesei or 'island in a marsh of a man called Beornmund' and it had become Bermunsesye by 1086.

## GEORGE INN, Borough High Street, SE1

One of the most famous pubs in London, this is a surviving coaching inn. Built in the 15th century as the St George, it was mentioned in 1598 as being in a pretty dreadful area of slums, brothels, stews and bear and dog fighting. Shakespeare took his troupe to act here. It was on a main coaching route and up to 100 coaches a week used it. With outstanding black and white frontage, Charles Dickens writes of it in *Little Dorritt*. It is haunted by shapes and temperature drops.

The landlord reports strange noises in the night and electric lights going on and off with no one nearby. In 1885 William Rendle wrote 'Bad news, the Restoration glory of this inn is departing, its fate sealed. It will soon be pulled down altogether.' In 1855 George Rymer hanged himself from the shaft of a wagon and has been haunting the courtyard and bars since. A former landlady, Miss Murray, is still in residence and creates havoc with computers and tills although nothing is wrong when checked by engineers. The 6th Lord Digby rescued people from Marchalsea Prison for debt by paying off creditors and taking them to the George for supper. Once he took 30 people. The present Old Bar is where coachmen and passengers waited for departure time. Often the name George refers to St George or indicates a royal connection. Since 1714 there have been six King Georges.

## GLOBE TAVERN, Bedale Street, SE1

In March 1807 a candle dropped in the bar started a fire that ripped through the old building. The landlord, his wife and five children escaped, but five lodgers out of 20 perished in the inferno. 'Several of the local buildings were much injured' according to reports. Some lodgers who died have since been seen dressed in old-fashioned clothing with one described as having a hideously burned face. Built on the site of an earlier pub in the Gothic Revival style in 1872, it was named after the Globe Theatre built by Richard and Cuthbert Burbage and Shakespeare in 1599, which held 2,000 people. The pub has been used for the films *Blue Ice* starring Michael Caine and Bob Hoskins and *Bridget Jones's Diary*.

A Victorian newspaper report of a riot nearby read: 'A scene of riot and outrage, not often exceeded in the borough of Southwark, took place when more than 2,000 Persons collected on the occasion. A public house in Black

Lion Street was almost demolished by an assemblage of the lower classes and two women and a man were shot.'

---

## KING'S ARMS, Newcomen Street, SE1

Many years ago this area was called Axe and Bottle Yard and the inn was named the same. In 1735 the yard was widened, and the pub was demolished and rebuilt as the King's Head. For a while the street was known as King Street until it became Newcomen Street. London Bridge was built between 1176 and 1209 and lasted until the 19th century. The great stone gate built in 1728 was demolished in 1780 and the coat of arms sold to a stonemason in Newcomen Street. It is still included in the inn sign for the renamed King's Arms.

## LORD CLYDE, Clenman Street, SE1

A pub has stood here for 300 years, but the old building was rebuilt in 1913

with a wealth of brass, mirrors and historical prints of the area. The exterior is earthware tiling in green and cream, dating from 1913 when the landlord, E.J. Taylor, moved in. His name remains alongside that of the brewer. There is a 1920s photograph of E.J. and an outgoing charabanc party. Lord Clyde, Sir Colin Campbell (1792–1863), a distinguished Field Marshall, was involved in the Relief of Lucknow, India, in 1857. An early landlord of this pub served under Lord Clyde there and named it after him.

## MARKET PORTER, Stoney Street, SE1

One of the oldest in pubs in Southwark, it has been here since 1638 and is one

of the few still open in the morning for market porters. Beer mats mounted on oak-panelled walls decorate the place and the floor is bare boards. There is some leaded glass and early 20th-century wall lamps. The pub has an up-market ghost who stands at the bar demanding cigars, but when staff turn around he has gone. Regularly they have trouble with

the place settings in the restaurant and cutlery is moved around or disappears. The landlord has found the till ringing up amounts after it has been emptied. On another occasion after he had turned off the glass-washing machine he found in the morning it had been turned back on and water was flooding the pub.

## OLD KING'S HEAD, King's Head Yard, SE1

During the problems between Henry VIII and Rome this pub was known as the Pope's Head. It seemed a good idea to keep on the side of royalty and it was swiftly renamed the King's Head. In 1560 the pub was part of the estate of Thomas Cure, Master of the Queen's Horse and founder of Cure College. He died in 1588 and it was bought by a Mr Humble whose family ran it for almost a century. There is an archway leading to a cobbled yard and during the summer the shutters open up onto the yard.

## ROYAL OAK, Tabard Street, SE1

This delightful pub would not be out of place in a country village. When Chaucer and his pilgrims left for Canterbury they would have felt comfortable in this bare boarded pub, once on the main road to Dover. (They left from the Tabard Inn, now long gone.) Outside are tiled walls with large old-fashioned lanterns. It is a two-bar pub with a 'bottle and jug' between bars, shelves of books and a brass foot rail. The name Royal Oak is second only to Red Lion in popularity. It celebrates the occasion when Charles II and Colonel Carless hid up an oak tree at Boscobel, when escaping from the Battle of Worcester in 1651.

The Wheatsheaf,
Stoney Street.

## WHEATSHEAF, Stoney Street, SE1

Now here is a two-bar inn to savour. Opposite Borough Market, it is a low ceilinged and bare boarded pub with no loud music, just conversation. For some curious reason the door to the men's lavatory carries a portrait of Jimi Hendrix and there is a woman on the ladies' whom I did not recognise. A most quaint addition is that of candles along a shelf in small basins for lighting cigarettes. The Wheatsheaf has been a popular pub name since the 17th century. It appears on several coats of arms including that of the Worshipful Company of Bakers since 1486 and is one of the devices on the arms of the Brewers' Company.

# Chapter 15
# HAMPSTEAD,
# HIGHGATE
# AND ARCHWAY

Upper Flask, now Flask in Highgate.

Archway Tavern,
Archway Road.

## ARCHWAY TAVERN, Archway Road, N6

Near here Dick Whittington looked back at the city and decided to return. Built in 1813, the same year as Jane Austen's *Pride and Prejudice* was published, it is where the Toxophilite Society, an association of archers, used to practise. It has a curved bar with carved pillars holding a coach-style clock. On Archway Hill is a statue of Whittington's cat, describing the man as Lord Mayor of London during the reigns of Richard II, Henry IV and Henry V, and Sheriff in 1392. Much has been made of his cat but the true story is that Whittington made a fortune from coal and the barges were called 'cats'. Slightly to the north of the pub over 200,000 people camped out to escape from the Great Fire of London of 1666.

## ASSEMBLY HOUSE, Kentish Town Road, NW5

This is an imposing 300-year-old inn where travellers gathered to board their coaches. It was noted for holding splendid balls in the 1750s and on gala nights it was lit up by numerous lamps. High ceilings are decorated with ornate plasterwork, which, I am told by a craftsman, would be almost impossible to do today.

## BULL AND BUSH, North End Way, NW3

Once a farmhouse, the earliest records of the pub go back to 1721 when Walpole became Prime Minister. It was frequented by writers William Hogarth, Charles Dickens and Wilkie Collins, and painters Gainsborough and

Reynolds. A fashionable area, it is still home to artists and writers. The theme song of Florrie Ford in the early 1900s 'Come, come, Come and make eyes at me, Down at the old Bull and Bush', refers to this pub. As a result of the popularity of this song thousands of cockneys took her at her word and flocked here.

## BULL AND LAST,
### Highgate Road, NW5

Stage coaches from the north called here and the coachmen cried, 'Bull and last' as the Bull Inn was the last stop before London. Now it is a late Victorian corner pub with very high ceilings and a chandelier, a three-sided bar and large windows with

etched glass. It is bareboarded but comfortable and includes a selection of works by a local photographer.

## DUKE OF HAMILTON, New End, NW3

A one-bar pub over two centuries old, it was named after one of the leading Royalists from the English Civil War. William, 2nd Duke of Hamilton, was Royalist Commander-in-Chief at the Battle of Worcester in 1651. He was shot in the thigh during an attack and was told the only cure was amputation. Cromwell, on the other side, offered his own surgeon to do the work but Hamilton refused. A month later he was dead from gangrene. At one time local inquests were held in the pub.

## FLASK, Flask Walk, NW3

In the 17th century six acres of land in Hampstead were left to the poor by the Hon. Susanna Noel. A spring ran down creating a pool and in 1689 trustees were set up to administer the charity. They increased their wealth by

advertising these as medicinal waters sold at threepence a flask. The water was collected, flasked and taken to this pub under its old name of Thatched House. Hampstead became a fashionable spa with many flocking there to take the waters. For many years the Flask was known as the Lower Flask to differentiate it from the Upper Flask. There was a thatched roof on the Flask as late as 1874 and an oyster bar until 1939. In the saloon bar there are panels painted by Jan van Beers. During renovation at the end of the 20th century the original 18th-century cellar walls were revealed. The main bar clock is stuck at 11 o'clock.

## FLASK IN HIGHGATE, Highgate West Hill, N6

A notable establishment built in 1663. The listed bar dates from 1716 and housed the Kit Kat Club of Sir Robert Walpole, England's first prime minister,

Pope, Swift and other famous characters. In 1748 in Samuel Richardson's novel, Clarissa Harlow took tea at the Upper Flask. She labels the 'Lower' Flask as where 'secondary characters are to be found in swinish condition'. There is nothing quite like being jilted or crossed in love

for a ghost to appear. Here a woman wanders wailing, crying and leaving cold spots behind. There are stories of a young woman who killed herself in unrequited love and she is connected with a portrait and a bullet hole in a wall. On occasions she has been seen moving glasses about on tables as though having a ouija session, and blowing down the necks of customers. There is a veritable warren of rooms here with flagstoned floors and open fires. Among past celebrities that drank here were William Hogarth, Karl Marx, John Betjeman and Dick Turpin. The pub is near Highgate Cemetery, where Marx is buried.

## FREEMASON'S ARMS, Downshire Hill, NW3

An impressive whitewashed pub, the Freemasons has one of the last 'pell mell' alleys left. This alleyway is now closed but the game involved rolling a large heavy wooden ball through iron hoops. Originally the freemasons were stonemasons who worked on cathedrals, churches and important buildings. They were proud of their crafts and used secret signs to keep out those of lesser talents or 'cowboy' builders. The Freemasons is now a well-known charitable organisation.

## HOLLY BUSH, Holly Mount, NW3

The pub is in a most delightful area, with wide steps up windy lanes. The inn is haunted by a waitress wearing a crisp apron or pinafore of linen. This has

upset customers, who insist on calling out that their food is taking too long and what does she know about it. Here she smiles wearily and disappears. There is another ghost here who pats the pianist on the shoulder now and again and whispers something they cannot hear. It is built on stables of the house of artist George Romney. Once there were seven bars, one the Coffee Bar, and they were used in their time by Dr Johnson and Boswell. During recent renovation the old gas lighting was condemned by the local council as unsafe.

It has been done up nicely using old wood and pieces from other pubs. Poetry readings are held here on Tuesday nights.

## OLD CROWN, Highgate Hill, N6

This fine confection is named after an old coin stamped with a crown, the last of which were worth 25 new pence, and is opposite the statue of Whittington's cat. It is the last remaining pub where the odd custom of 'swearing of the horns' was carried out. Coaching passengers heading south and north would be invited to take the Highgate Oath at this and other pubs. This included bringing in the horns on a pole five feet long and placing them upright in front of the person to be sworn. It also involved buying several bottles of wine

and then as Freemen of Highgate, being told 'If at any time you are going through the hamlet and want to rest yourself and see a pig lying in the ditch you are quite at liberty to kick her out and take her place. But if you see three lying together you must only kick out the middle one and lie between the two. So, God Save the King.'

## SPANIARD'S INN, Spaniard's Road, NW3

This is an old inn on Hampstead Heath where that ubiquitous highwayman, Dick Turpin, hid guns. From time to time he is still seen to leave the inn and gallop across the heath on a black horse, wearing a black coat. There is a myth that this inn was the birthplace of Turpin in 1705. Not true; he was born many miles to the north at Hempstead in Essex where his father was landlord of the

Blue Bell. He might well have stabled his horse, Black Bess, at the old toll-gate opposite. A shadowy figure is often seen striding towards the bar before disappearing into the wall. Poet John Keats was o'ertaken by the muse here and ran up 'Ode to a Nightingale'. Other poets, Goldsmith and Byron, were habitués and the pub is mentioned in Dickens's *Pickwick Papers* and Bram Stoker's *Dracula*.

## WILLIAM IV, Hampstead, NW3

There are two ghosts at this pub named after the Sailor King. One is a young girl wearing a long white dress or nightgown with long hair in plaits, and her unhappy face is seen looking through the windows on the first floor. The story runs that she committed suicide in a dental surgery opposite the pub. The other ghost lived at the pub many years ago and was murdered by her husband then walled up. She ensures people know she is still about by loud wailings with the shaking of windows and banging of inside doors during the night.

## YE OLDE WHITE BEAR, Well Road, NW3

Like an old-fashioned club for comfort, with shuttered windows and two bars,

there is wood block flooring throughout this pub with some good pieces of furniture including an Edwardian sideboard. The walls are dark green and red and there is a cosy bar. Wood panelling and signed photographs and letters from local actors and writers who have used it over the years decorate the walls. Outside is a seating area with old-fashioned street lights in one of the most protected environments in London. The white bear was an heraldic device of the earls of Kent and the name of a galleon built in 1563 that was part of Drake's squadron at Cadiz.

# *Chapter 16*
# CITY AND EAST
# LONDON

Until the 1400s east London was green fields and farms, but two centuries later it was slaughter-houses, fish farms, leather tanners and breweries. Since 1650 there has been a huge influx of immigrants. London docks grew up between London Bridge and the Tower of London. This led to chronic overcrowding and lawlessness on a grand scale with murder and robbery a daily occurrence. In the unlit alleyways between the tenements the women would work as prostitutes. George Gissing described it as 'the city of the damned'.

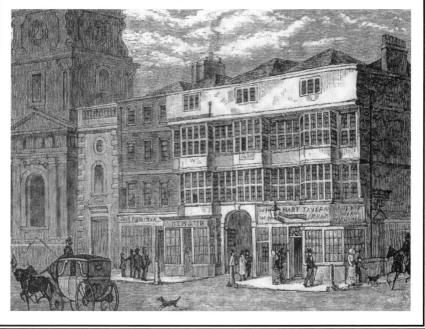

Pearly Kings and Queens started with an orphan, Henry Croft. He shared the same birth date as Queen Victoria and dressed up in finery to share some of her fame and glory. He decorated his clothing with huge numbers of pearl buttons and others copied him. Nowadays the 'pearlies' work for charity.

Philosophers and political thinkers lived in the area, including Stalin, who lived near the Whitechapel Bell Foundry, where the 13-ton Big Ben and the American Liberty Bell were cast. Marx's daughter, Eleanor, took part in the 1889 dock strike. The fifth Congress of the Russian Social Democratic Labour Party took place in Fulbourne Street in May 1907 and was attended by Lenin, Stalin, Trotsky, Litnova and Gorky.

Smithfield Market was a place of execution for 400 years. Witches, heretics and religious martyrs were hanged or burned alive. Here all the debris from the Great Fire of London was piled up. *Four Weddings and a Funeral* was part filmed at St Bartholmew's Church.

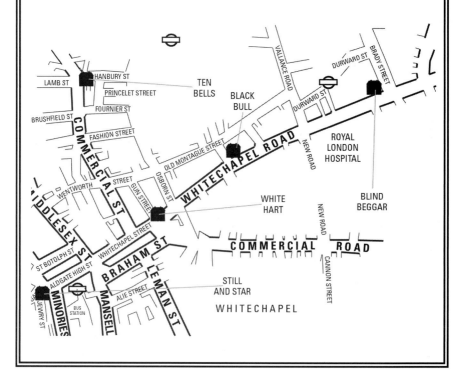

## ANCHOR TAP,
### Horsleydown Lane, SE1

Pubs with this name are connected with 'anker', an old name for eight and a half imperial gallons of beer. The pub is close to Tower Bridge and has a resident ghost. Occasionally things appear and disappear and because he has been around so long the ghost has been nicknamed Charlie. One of his larks is to smash ashtrays in the middle of the night and play around with sound systems. Once a woman's watch disappeared from her bedroom and reappeared eight weeks later in a laundry basket. Inside this 18th-century former dockers' pub is plenty of dark wood panelling. Brewing in Southwark is mentioned by Chaucer and in Horsleydown by Shakespeare. Samuel Johnson stayed here when compiling his dictionary.

## BLACK BULL, Whitechapel Road, E1

A fine black and white-timbered pub that would be at home in any country

village. It has one large bar for locals and actors from the nearby theatre. There is an eclectic mix of decorative artifacts: riding boots, old whisky bottles, an old clock, cider casks and framed details of a Wreck Sale (goods salvaged from ships wrecked on the coast or in the Thames) and the Glorious Victory of Lord Nelson at Gibraltar. It is divided into railed alcoves and an enormous brass fan whirls above seating areas. Outside is the bustling market. The area was known as Whitechapele in 1340, from a white stone-built chapel.

## BLACK LION, High Street, E13

A 16th-century coaching inn with bare wood floors and antiques. The colour black was commonly used as a pub description in the 18th century. When the Gin Act was imposed in 1736 it meant higher taxes and many licensees draped their inn signs with black velvet and added the name 'black' to show their disapproval. The Black Lion was another inn where Dick Turpin plied his trade.

## BLIND BEGGAR, Whitechapel Road, E1

The original blind beggar is told of in a story of the Battle of Evesham in 1265,

when the son of a noble escaped disguised as a blind beggar and got to London. There Henry, son of Simon de Montfort, traveled around as a beggar amassing a fortune which he gave to his daughter on her wedding day. However, this pub was named after a ballad, *The Blind Beggar of Bethnal Green.* It is a large inn with a horseshoe-shaped bar in the centre and old and comfortable armchairs and sofas. The first sermon by General Booth of the Salvation Army was preached outside and in 1865 the Salvation Army

was selling *War Cry* and trying to persuade men to give up the evil drink. It has since gained a more sinister reputation as it is where Ronnie Kray shot George Cornell.

## BOW BELLS, Bow Road, E3

They treat their ghost here as a feature of the pub and have a warning sign over the door to the ladies' lavatory. This mischievous apparition has been known to flush the loo at most inappropriate times. A number of women reporting the 'phantom flusher' say that the door bursts open and a curious force flushes the cistern. One landlord who saw a strange mist arising from the toilet floor organised a seance. During this seance there was a loud smash on the door and a window-pane shattered. It is not named after the Bow Bells of nursery rhyme fame.

## BRIDGE HOUSE, Tower Bridge Road, SE1

Once there were many small pubs around the Tower but all have disappeared. This is curious, because of the volume of tourists. The only other pub nearby is the Pommeller's Rest at the end of the bridge. Very little is known of the history of Bridge House, but the name Pommeller's refers to saddle makers, and there is a history of leather workers in the area.

## CAPTAIN KIDD, Wapping High Street, E1

Captain Kidd was hanged for piracy, murder and treason in 1701 after a trial in the Houses of Parliament. He was born in Scotland and by 1690 was established as a ship owner in colonial New York. In 1695 he was commissioned as a privateer to act against pirates. In 1699 a warrant was issued for his arrest and he returned to England to defend his honour. He abandoned his ship, the *Quedagh Merchant*, in the West Indies, laden with treasure that has never been found. The pub is entered through a cobbled passageway where facts about Kidd's life are hung on brick walls. It is stone-flagged with large wooden beams and barrels used as tables. When Kidd was hanged the first rope broke but the second did its job. His body was left so that three tides washed over him and was then hung in chains as a warning to other pirates. Outside there is a riverside patio with palm trees.

## FERRY HOUSE, Ferry Street, E14

This is the oldest pub on the Isle of Dogs. There was a ferry between Greenwich and the Isle of Dogs and this was the ferry-master's house before

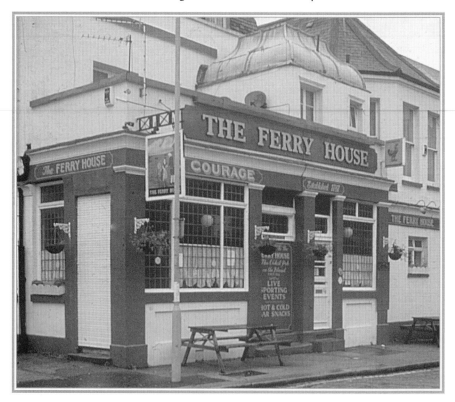

they built a foot tunnel under the Thames. There was an alehouse on this site 500 years ago and the area was referred to as Isle of Dogs Ferm in 1593, which meant a marshy area frequented by wild dogs. Another story is that Charles II kept his hunting dogs here when he lived at Greenwich Palace. An historian maintains it was once the Isle of Ducks. Pepys's reference, 'We were fain to stay there in the unlucky Isle of Dogs in a chill place to our great discontent' gave rise to the phrase 'going to the dogs'.

## GRAPES, Narrow Street, E14

An ancient pub rooted firmly in the 16th century with good rich panelling and great views overlooking the Thames. It suffered from fire and other disasters and was rebuilt in 1720. At the rear is a veranda on stilts over the water used by artists to paint the river. Dickens knew it well and described it in *Our Mutual Friend* as the Six Jolly Fellowship Porters and 'A tavern of a

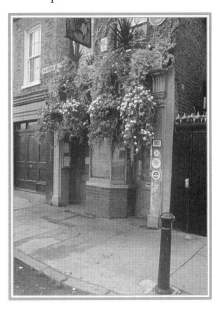

dropsical appearance that had long settled down into a state of hale infirmity. In its whole construction it had not a straight floor and hardly a straight line; but it had outlasted, and clearly would outlast, many a better trimmed building, many a sprucer public house.' There was a gruesome trade locally when watermen rowed drunks out onto the river, drowned them and sold their bodies to surgeons for practice. It was built in 1580–81 as Sir Francis Drake completed the first English circumnavigation of the world and Roman Catholics smuggled in priests to support a persecuted faith. There is a fine oil painting of the Grapes and some customers painted in 1949 by Alice West.

## GUN INN, Coldharbour, E14

Once many inns were called the Gun but that is not so today. Gun or Cannon pubs have heraldic connections with Edward IV, Queen Mary and Queen Elizabeth I. The wooden ceilings at this pub are decorated with many naval flags, some signed by ships' crews. The uneven plaster walls carry photographs including Shackleton's expedition to the Antarctic and a

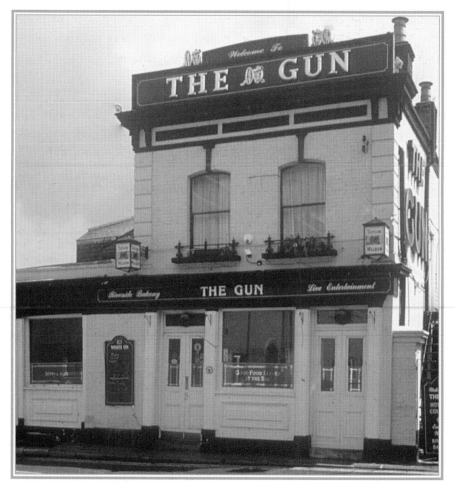

clock set within a ship's wheel, and there is a terrace with splendid views across the river. In 1716 it was called the King and Queen, then it became the Rose and Crown, then the Ramsgate Pink and finally the Gun in 1770. There is a spyhole in a door dating from the Napoleonic Wars, to make sure the coast was clear of revenue men when smugglers were about. A room above is called Lady Hamilton, as she and Lord Nelson met here and at nearby Nelson House before his forays abroad. It is haunted by Lord Nelson, who is described as a small man in naval uniform wearing a tricorne hat.

## HOOP AND GRAPES, Aldgate High Street, EC3

This is the only timber-framed pub left that escaped the Fire of London. Flames got within 50 yards and it was later decided there should be no more new timber-framed buildings. It was built in 1598, two years before the birth of Charles I and the year of the founding of the East India Company. Since then it has been called the Castle, Angel and Crown and Christopher Hills, becoming the Hoop and Grapes in 1920. In 1666 the landlord was Robert Taylor. It has a long wide bar with exposed brickwork, massive support beams, stone flags and is decorated with old photographs. Built on three storeys, with a garret and a cellar containing the lavatories, it has exposed brick arches. There was a mediaeval tunnel to the Convent of St Clare in the Minories, the Tower of London and the Thames, that was used by smugglers. After the Great Fire insurance companies set up and

each company had its own sign that traders placed in their windows. In the 1980s the Hoop and Grapes was refurbished and underpinned with a steel skeleton to support the ancient building. In the Conan Doyle novels Sherlock Holmes told Dr Watson, 'Always carry a pistol east of Aldgate' because it was such a dangerous area.

## LAMB TAVERN, Leadenhall Market, EC3

This is a listed building from 1780 with a wealth of engraved glass. A tiled picture shows Sir Christopher Wren with the plans for the Monument, and depicts the Pudding Lane fire that started the Great Fire of London of 1666. It started in the house and shop of Thomas Farynour, the King's baker. He and his family escaped through a window but a maidservant, too scared to climb through, perished. She was the first victim of the fire that raged for five days. There has been continuous occupation here since the Romans arrived so now

Lamb Tavern,
Leadenhall Market.

roads and houses are built on old roads that have disappeared into history. Leadenhall was built in 1309 by Sir Hugh Neville with a large roof of lead, hence the name: Leadenhall. In 1666 it was badly damaged and rebuilt as a market for butchers and fishmongers. The Lamb is on top of a Roman basilica. It was a well-known coaching inn for businessmen visiting shipping offices in Leadenhall Street to make arrangements for shipping goods or booking passage for themselves abroad.

## NEW MOON, Leadenhall Market, EC3

Opened in 1736, the same year as the repeal of statutes against witchcraft, this is a large L-shaped pub with bare boards and a traditional bar counter along its length. Although witchcraft trials ceased after this date the last one was in 1944 against Helen Duncan who, as a medium, divulged World War Two secrets and was jailed. The act was finally repealed in 1951.

## OLD DR BUTLER'S HEAD, Mason's Avenue, Coleman Street, EC2

Although never qualified as a doctor of medicine, Dr William Butler became

court physician to James I. The king was persuaded to see him because of agonising back pain and Butler gave him a prodding and made up a special alcoholic brew that kept the pain at bay. The good doctor was as odd as his patient, who once knighted a Loin of Beef, which then had a pub named after it. The king, described as 'the wisest fool in Christendom', arranged an honorary degree for the doctor. Butler's cure for sufferers from epilepsy was to let off a brace of pistols without warning to shock them out of it. More of a medicinal lark was to throw plague sufferers into a chilly pool. The pub was built in 1616 by Butler as part of a small empire of properties in the area. With low beams and a wooden floor it is one of the treasures of London.

## SPOTTED DOG INN, Upton Lane, London E7

An interesting pub in east London, the Spotted Dog has connections with Henry VII and VIII and Anne Boleyn, and was a coaching inn in the 16th century. King Henry kept hunting dogs nearby and met up with Anne Boleyn

when visiting Westham Palace. It is the oldest secular building in the area and was built as a timber-framed high-vaulted building over 500 years ago. There are stone flags throughout with Victorian fireplaces and a large plaster statue of Henry and the spotted dog. There are low beams in the upstairs restaurant. The spotted dog refers to the Dalmatian dog that the fashionable set had racing along by their coaches. It was granted a 24-hour licence by Charles II. From 1603 city merchants used it as their local Exchange and the name, City Arms, was painted onto one wall that can still be seen. Dick Turpin is said to have used the inn when he was a butcher at Eastham.

## PRINCE ARTHUR, Forest Road, E8

For 15 years this Victorian corner pub was known as the Lady Diana and was the only pub named after a member of the royal family who was still alive. It was named two months before she became Princess Diana. But things do change and it is now called the Prince Arthur, after the third son of Queen Victoria. When I turned up the landlord was outside painting it. Asked about the change of name he said that there comes a point when even the most famous people lose their attraction as a pub name.

## PROSPECT OF WHITBY, Wapping Wall, E1

One of London's best-known pubs, it is named after an old coaler that plied between London and Whitby. A more genteel crowd gather here today, not like the days when it was called the 'Devil's Tavern' because of the riff-raff, smugglers and evildoers who used it. Built in 1520 from a timber-framed

country house, it was constructed at the same time as the Field of the Cloth of Gold conference between King Henry VIII and Francis I of France. Among those who visited it were Pepys and Judge Jeffreys. Samuel Pepys was Secretary to the Admiralty during the reign of Charles II and attended here on naval business. The room he used for dining is now called Ye Pepys. Jeffreys came to watch the hangings of sailors that took place below low-water mark, where the bodies were left for three tides. A macabre noose still hangs over the river on the terrace. It was said that Jeffreys was captured here hiding in the cellars disguised as a coal heaver, but this is not true. It was at the Town of Ramsgate pub in Wapping High Street, and he was disguised as a sailor. One customer was John Westcome, who returned from Japan in 1780 and exchanged a flower he obtained there for a glass of rum. Market gardener Mr Lea grew 300 cuttings from this plant, which became the fuchsia. There is a stone-flagged bar with a pewter bar top and a terrace overlooking the River Thames.

## QUEEN'S HEAD, Flamborough Street, E14

For centuries this was a popular pub name but Queen Elizabeth I objected to some of the terrible inn signs that went up in her image. Inspectors were sent out to investigate and poorly executed signs were knocked down and burned in the street. In 1563 there was a Royal Proclamation that maintained all landlords should follow an approved example: namely that they flattered the Virgin Queen. Since Saxon times there has been a village here and this Queen's Head was built on land owned by Henry Colet, a merchant and Mayor of London who died in 1505. In July 1987 it was visited by Elizabeth, the Queen Mother. She pulled a pint and this became one of the most famous of all royal pictures.

## SALMON AND BALL, Cambridge Heath Road, E2

Dating from 1733, the pub was named the Salmon and then Ball was added

because mercers used the inn and the reference was to a ball of silk. In the Cutter's Riots of 1769 local silk weavers went on strike for more wages and slashed the silk from the looms already working. In the riot to arrest the leaders three people died and two were arrested to be hanged outside the Salmon and Ball. The two, John Doyle and John Valline, are said to haunt the pub. At the end of the 19th century it was a meeting place for the Socialist League and in the 1930s Oswald Mosley and his Fascists. Inside are photographs of East End boxers and the sign 'The road to the bog' is also in Irish Gaelic.

## STILL AND STAR, Little Somerset Street, E1

This is the only pub with this name, which comes from the still used for distilling. In late Victorian days there were many slaughterhouses and

butchers in east London to avoid taxes further into the city. Because of this the pub came under the watchful eye of the police in 1888 as it was thought Jack the Ripper could be a slaughterman that worked here. There is a long narrow bar with stained-glass windows, horse brasses and an open fire with brass grate. There is a list of landlords going back to 1870 and on the gable wall is a door and winching hoist.

## TEN BELLS, Commercial Street, E1

Some of Jack the Ripper's five victims drank here before plying their trade and he probably drank here as well, keeping an eye on potential victims. One victim, Annie Chapman, was seen leaving the Ten Bells the night she was slain and at Hanbury Street her ghost still walks. In the bar of the Ten Bells, built in

1753, the same year the British Museum was opened, there are ancient newspaper cuttings and pictures reporting the grisly deeds. It is near Brick Lane, home to Asian traders, and Petticoat Lane. On the opposite corner is Christ Church, built in 1714 by Nicholas Hawksmoor.

## THREE LORDS, The Minories, EC3

The pub was originally built over 300 years ago on a street named after the Convent of the Little Sisters of St Clare, the Sorores Minores, founded in 1293. It is named after three Jacobite Lords loyal to Bonnie Prince Charlie and beheaded for their part in the uprising on Tower Hill. They were the Earl of Kilmarnock, Lord Lovat and Lord Balmerino. Two bars are still named 'The '45' and 'Culloden'. When rebuilt in 1894 it was praised in the *City Press* for its stained-glass windows, mosaic pavements, encaustic tiles and cut-glass panels. Bonnie Prince Charlie escaped in September 1746 on the French ship *L'Heureux* from Arisaig and died in Rome a broken man in 1788. There are tales and legends of a large amount of gold raised to help the Young Pretender buried near Loch Arkaig, Scotland, where it probably still lies.

## TOWN OF RAMSGATE, Wapping High Street, E1

This is a long narrow pub running down to the river with steps to the water.

Judge Jeffreys was caught outside the pub trying to escape, disguised as a sailor, on board a collier bound for Hamburg. He was recognised by a scrivener who had appeared before him. Jeffreys was recognised although he had shaved off his heavy eyebrows. Rescued by a patrol of Trained Bands he died in the Tower of London aged 40. (Trained Bands were companies of militia set up by James I to control local disorders, which afterwards became the London Militia.) The pub was once known as the Red Cow, after a barmaid who worked there. Press-ganged men were held here before being sent out to ships, as well as men being transported to the colonies. A picture of Ramsgate Harbour dated 1850 features on the inn sign. It changed to the Town of Ramsgate when Ramsgate fishermen landed their wares here. In 1789 the Marine Police were set up in Wapping High Street and, as the world's first regular police force, patrolled the river in rowing boats to prevent theft from boats anchored midstream.

## TURNER'S OLD STAR, Watts Street, E1

This one-roomed pub was so named because the painter, William Turner, bought it and gave it to one of his mistresses, Sophia Booth. Occasionally he

visited Sophia at the pub and called himself Mr Booth. Turner was a short, fat man known locally as Puggy Booth. Turner owned two other pubs in the area, the Ship and the Bladebone. Nearby is Reardon Street where Captain William Bligh lived in 1785. He was the captain of the ill-fated *Bounty* that sailed for Tahiti in 1787 and there is a blue plaque on the building.

## WHITE HART, Bishopsgate, EC2

This pub was old when Shakespeare lived nearby and is mentioned in several of his plays. It was on the drovers' route from the eastern counties and the present building is mid-Victorian, standing next to St Botolph's church. Bishopsgate was named after a Saxon bishop in the eighth century. Around the corner is the Railway Tavern, also on the old drover's route, and still nicknamed 'the Cowshed'.

## WHITE HART, Gunthorpe Street, E1

On the corner of Gunthorpe Street and an eerie alleyway, this pub was known to Jack the Ripper and his victims. A notice on the wall says it is haunted by a weeping woman dressed in Victorian-style clothing. One of the Ripper's victims, Martha Turner, had her last drink here before being murdered. George Chapman, a barber-surgeon who lived in the cellars of this pub, was arrested as a suspect and later hanged. (Well, he had poisoned three wives, but was he Jack the Ripper?) Built in 1721, the bar runs the length of the pub. The white hart is a popular sign adopted by Richard II in 1377, the same year as the first Poll Tax and the first Speaker in the House of Commons. (The first English cook book, written for Richard II, included loseyn, pronounced lasan, a cheese and noodle dish now known as lasagne.) Nearby Dick Turpin shot dead a law officer after being tracked down in 1739.

## WIDOW'S SON, Devons Road, E3

Every Good Friday a hot cross bun is added to a collection going back 200 years. It started when the son of a woman licensee disappeared on his first trip to sea. She cooked him an Easter bun each year until she died. In the bar the buns still await him and tradition has it that the first sailor to go into the bar on Good Friday adds a new one. This has become so much part of East End

history that it is in the lease of the pub. During World War Two the buns were taken away for safe-keeping. Superstition has it that buns baked on Good Friday will never go stale and can be used as a medicine in certain illnesses. The pub is known as the Bun House. (The Widow's Son is a term used by Freemasons and is an old phrase referring to Jesus as the widow's son.) At nearby Glaucus Street there used to be a ducking stool for dipping difficult and troublesome women in the local pond and it was still in use in the early 1800s. The ducking stool was used test witches by tying them to it and sinking them into water. If they drowned they were innocent, if they floated they were guilty.

# *Chapter 17*
# GREENWICH

**CUTTY SARK,** Ballast Quay, SE10

An early 19th-century pub with splendid views over the Thames. Known as the Union Tavern in 1804, it changed in 1954 when the 19th-century clipper *Cutty Sark* was laid up in dry dock and opened to the public. The Cutty Sark pub is in a row of early 19th-century town houses including the Harbourmaster's Office. The front is a large bowed window curving out on the upper floor and inside there are bare floorboards and a mantelpiece made from old ship's timbers. Cutty sark was the name given to the roughly woven shirts worn in the border region of Scotland and is the name of the witch in *Tam o' Shanter*. Greenwich was called Grenewic in AD 964 and Grenwiz in 1086, and translates as 'green port or harbour'. Ballast Quay was named because it was where gravel was shipped in the 17th century. Following the Great Fire of London insurance companies were set up and nearby are fire insurance plaques.

**PILOT INN,** River Way, SE10

Set at the end of a row of Victorian cottages is the dashing early Victorian Pilot Inn. It is behind a modern cobbled square and has a nautical look that does not surprise, as most Pilot Inns are connected with boats and ships. It has a long main bar and bare boards, with rooms going off for restaurants and a children's room. At the rear is an attractive beer garden with tables and chairs. Decorations are mainly of a nautical nature with ship's wheels and plates behind the bar, as well as painted sailing ships. It was established in 1801, the same year as the first census was made in Britain.

## PLUME OF FEATHERS, Park Vista, SE10

Sitting on the Meridian Line, the Plume is over three centuries old and is one of the oldest pubs in Greenwich. Usually this sign refers to the plume of three feathers adopted as a crest by the Black Prince and King John of Hungary, who charged at the Battle of Poitiers in 1356 with the cry of 'Ich Dien ('I serve'). There are also common beliefs about feathers being personal decoration at times of valour. In primitive tribes there is the custom of adding a feather to one's headdress after killing an enemy. In English the expression, 'There's a feather in your cap' means someone has done well.

## RICHARD I, Royal Hill, SE10

Over 600 years ago Greenwich was a fishing village with a royal residence and Edward I, Henry VIII and Elizabeth I were born there. There were two annual fairs here and large numbers of Londoners turned out for the day. To feed these hordes a number of taverns and alehouses opened their doors to them. What a splendid address the pub has – Royal Hill – but it was known as Gang Lane over 200 years ago. That was because navy press gangs raided the streets and pubs looking for men to sail the ships. Richard I was Richard the Lionheart (1157–1199) and reigned from 1189. He went on the Third Crusade in 1190 and was out of the country for most of his reign, being taken prisoner and ransomed. The pub was originally two shops, one of them selling ale and beers, which later became Ye Olde House. It is a traditional pub with no music, TV or gaming machines, and there are bare wooden boards throughout the two bars.

## SPANISH GALLEON, Greenwich Church Street, SE10

This pub was built in the reign of William IV, the Sailor King. When renovated in 1985 a bricked-up room was found in the cellars and inside was a well-preserved sailor's uniform of the 19th century, when ships were changing from sail to steam power. That uniform is now in the Galleon Bar. There is history that suggests that there were previous inns, also called the Galleon, on the same site for perhaps 200 years before the present building. There have been reports over the years of hauntings in the bars and cellars and some poltergeist activity.

## TRAFALGAR TAVERN, Park Row, SE10

A noble, impressive inn overlooking the river, the Trafalgar Tavern was an alehouse as early as the 11th century. The current pub was built in 1837, with large bowed windows and wrought-iron balconies, by Joseph Keys, Surveyor of Greenwich Hospital. For years it provided shore living quarters for sailors. Greenwich was famous for whitebait suppers, the small fry of herring. Politicians flocked to Greenwich for these fish feasts and the Trafalgar housed the Liberals while the Conservatives met at the long-gone Ship until the 1890s. These dinners now take place as the annual charitable Ministerial Whitebait Dinner in the Regency banqueting hall. Charles Dickens mentions the Trafalgar in *Little Dorritt* and was a regular visitor. Some years ago a barman saw an elderly man in Victorian dress near the piano on an upstairs floor, who has been seen on many occasions since. One landlady got so used to him that she greeted him with a cheerful 'Hello and good morning'. Beer crates have moved about in the cellars while staff have been working there. The pub has four inter-connecting rooms and is decorated with naval memorabilia.

## FIVE IDLERS OF PLUMSTEAD

The area of Plumstead in south-east London is an ancient one and dates back to Saxon times. It was known as Plumstede in AD 961 and Plumestede by 1086. It simply means a 'place where the plum trees grow'. Around Plumstead Common are five pubs, which are known as a group as the 'Five Idlers of

Plumstead'. All are early Victorian and idle because: the Star doesn't shine in the sky, the Woodman does not cut trees, the Ship cannot sail the seas, the Old Mill doesn't grind corn and the Prince never reigned.

# *Chapter 18*
# OTHER LONDON
# INNS AND TAVERNS

Mother Red Cap, now World's End, N1.

## ANGEL, High Street, SW15

Opened in the 17th century, this pub started life selling beer to travellers about the same time as Shakespeare died and Sir Walter Raleigh was executed. The first record of it is 1617, but it has been there much longer. The angel reflected the connections between monasteries and travellers' hostels. Some pubs called the Angel also referred to the gold coin called an 'angel noble', first minted in 1465, which lasted three centuries. In 1861 this was a wooden building with stables, coach houses and a bowling green. It was rebuilt in 1893. It has a wrought-iron entrance with a stained-glass angel and the inn sign shows a busty barmaid.

## BREWERY TAP, Wandsworth High Street, SW18

Dating from 1675 when the Royal Observatory at Greenwich was founded by Charles II, the pub was known as the Ram. By 1690 it was the Rame at Wansworth, and appears in a list of taverns 'In the contry 10 miles rond London'. It was badly damaged by fire in 1882 and again by bombs in World War Two.

## CAMDEN HEAD, Camden Walk, N1

A grandiose building overlooking Camden Passage market, this was a rehearsal pub for the Kinks pop group. It is another fine example of Victorian

opulence and even after restoration keeps many of the period features. Surrounded by acid-etched glass windows there is an ornate island bar and Edwardian lamps. Red velvet drapes and patterned carpets create a theatrical atmosphere. The area is named after Charles Pratt, 1st Earl of Camden (1714–94), who became Lord Chancellor. He owned the land that became Camden Town.

## CASTLE, Battersea High Street, SW11

There is an Elizabethan wooden carved sign here at the Castle, which was originally built in 1600. Battersea was famous for asparagus growing, brought here by the Huguenots. The sign was rediscovered in 1950 hidden under many coats of paint. The pub was a coaching inn with a first-floor bay window from which passengers climbed straight from the top of the coach.

## CRANE, Armoury Way, SW18

Over 250 years old, the Crane is named after either the bird or hoisting machinery. Occasionally the ghost of a boy of about 10 years old is seen wandering through wearing old-fashioned knickerbockers and a cap. Once there were many workshops and factories on the nearby River Wandle using lifting cranes in their business. Originally there were three bars here – one was the 'bottle and jug' for off sales – but now there are two bars. In 1832 it boasted a skittle alley. The first record of Wandsworth is as Wandele in the Domesday Book of 1086, and it meant an enclosure belonging to a man called Waendel.

## CROCKER'S FOLLY, Aberdeen Place, NW8

Over a century ago landlord Frank Crocker built a magnificent pub with lots of marble, archways, a noble fireplace and a display of glass and woodwork. There is even a carved bust of the Roman emperor, Caracalla, noted for his love of exotic architecture. Then hordes of people were pouring into London and Crocker thought the railway would arrive outside his front door, bringing

a roaring trade. But it did not happen, and Crocker jumped from a top-floor window to his demise. The pub has changed over the years and although it is not so grandiose as it was, it is making a profit. Crocker has been seen late in the evening when the takings are being counted. They do say his eyes are mad with envy. Designed by C.H. Worley, the building was originally called the Crown Hotel. In its heyday there were several bars including a 'bottle and jug' and a 'ladies only' bar.

## CROOKED BILLET, Crooked Billet, SW19

Excavations of a Roman camp on the common show that there was an Iron Age community here and this pub was first mentioned in 1509 as a brewery and inn. It had close connections with the Cromwell family and Walter Cromwell was a smith, armourer and hostelry keeper who took over the Crooked Billet in 1513 and died there in 1516. His son, Thomas, rose to become Lord High Chamberlain to Henry VIII. The first building has gone and in 1776 it was rebuilt on another site. In Edwards's *Companion from London to Brighthelmston* (Brighton) of 1789 it is described as a beerhouse.

## DOG AND FOX, Wimbledon High Street, SW18

The inn was used in the late 1700s and early 1800s as a headquarters for volunteers training to fight Napoleon if he ever landed in England. The area around the High Street was used as a fairground but became so licentious that the good burghers closed it down in 1840. In 1600 the pub was known as the Sign of My Lord's Arms and Inn, by Wimbledon Pound.

## DUKE OF CUMBERLAND, New King's Road, SW6

Named after Ernest Augustus, son of George III, this pub was once known as the Duke's Head. Before that it was called the Ponds End Tavern, having been built in 1657. Before the Restoration, King's Road was a country lane through market gardens and farms. In 1660 it was opened as a coach road as a direct route between Hampton Court and St James's Palace. Daily tickets were issued for commoners until 1830.

## EAGLE TAVERN, Shepherdess Walk, N1

The address, Shepherdess Walk, indicates that this was once a rural area. This Eagle is featured in the nursery rhyme: 'Up and down the City Road, In and out the Eagle, That's the way the money goes. Pop goes the weasel'. Once there were many tailors in City Road and the employees were poorly paid. They used to 'pop' or pawn their 'weasel' or working iron to buy beer. Nearby Ben Jonson killed the actor Gabriel Spencer in a duel in 1598. The tavern is built on the site of a Victorian theatre and pleasure garden and is near the old Britannia Theatre. The legendary Marie Lloyd made her first public appearance here in 1885 and there is a blue plaque to commemorate this.

## GILPIN'S BELL, Fore Street, N18

The pub is named after the linen draper and Trained Band captain, John

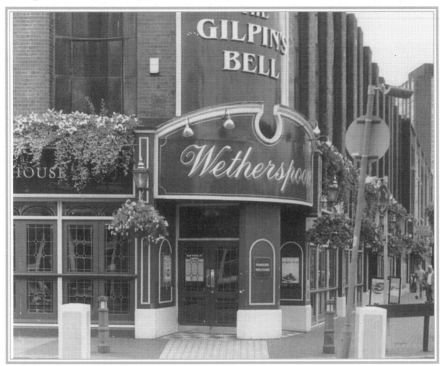

Gilpin, a character in a comic poem of 1785 by Cowper. After public readings of the poem by John Henderson it sold in its thousands. It was at the Bell that Gilpin and his unlucky spouse should have dined, but for the vagaries of fate. The name gradually changed from the Bell, to the Bell and Johnny Gilpin's

Ride, to Gilpin's Bell. It is a vast modern pub with modern stained-glass windows featuring a bell and hanging portraits of royalty and politicians. In the 1850s it was so famous, that, according to *Social Gleanings*, some Americans named the two places most worth a visit as St Paul's Cathedral and the Bell at Edmonton. (The story of Gilpin may have been based on a poem by Sir Thomas More, 'The Merry Jests of the Sergeant and Freere'.) The inn opened over 400 years ago. Edmonton was Adelmetone in 1086, meaning the farmstead of a man called Eadhelm.

## GREEN MAN, Putney Heath, SW15

Putney Heath was well known for duelling and many aristocrats and army officers were killed near the Green Man. It was a noted centre for highwaymen

165

Green Man,
Putney Heath.

and Dick Turpin hid guns in this pub. Protector Cromwell had distant relations in Putney, one of whom ran this pub, and in 1647 he stationed his New Model Army there. The Green Man is over 300 years old, and there are records of an earlier pub, the Anchor. The two original bars are small with wooden floors and half-panelled walls. Robbers and highwaymen used to lurk here to espy the rich travellers worth holding up on the heath. One was Jerry Abeshaw, born at Kingston and leader of a gang that terrorised people for miles around and killed Bow Street Runners and a pub landlord. When tried at Croydon Assizes in 1795 he put his own cap on when the judge put on his black cap to sentence him. After being hanged he was gibbeted at Putney with a place named after him, Jerry's Hill. A more salubrious gentleman was the poet Swinburne, who lived in Putney. Some chairs used by Swinburne and his friends are still in use.

## GOURAMYS, Cross Street, SW13

Opened 150 years ago for local market gardeners and railway workers, the pub was, until recently, called the Rose of Denmark after Alexandra, Princess of Wales, from Denmark, who set up Alexandra Rose Day in 1912 to celebrate 50 years of living here. Now it is a fish restaurant/pub named after a fish, the gouramy, which has a place of honour between the restaurant and bar. It is well worth a visit for the food and good beer.

## HARE AND HOUNDS, Upper Richmond Road, SW14

A fine roadside inn with a Georgian-style porch, this has been the Hare and Hounds since 1776; the same year as the Declaration of Independence by the American colonies. In the early years it was a coaching inn and a billet for regular soldiers. With only a few large houses and estates in the area there was a pack of hounds kept nearby. There used to be a crown bowling green here and stables for local polo players. There is a good public bar and another large bar through a separate entrance with billiard tables.

## KING'S ARMS, Peckham Rye, SE13

During World War Two the King's Arms received a direct hit from a German bomb that flattened the place and killed 11 people. Since then several of the dead have appeared accompanied by sounds of old-time music played on a piano coming from the cellars. Those who hear it say it is 'Roll out the barrel'. Many have seen people in old-fashioned clothing in the bar and cellar. There are reports of a Roman centurion being seen in one bar, and the word 'piano' was carved into the leg of a grand piano when no one was about. At one time there were 50 pubs named the King's Arms in London alone. On one pub sign Charles II was portrayed with his arms around Nell Gwynne. This gave rise to a merry jest that if you wanted a quiet drink you should go to the King's Head, because it was always empty, while the King's Arms was always full.

### KING'S HEAD, Roehampton, SW15

This is a large pub dating from 1485, when Richard III was defeated and killed at Bosworth and the Yeoman of the Guard was formed. Some King's Heads were run by Roundhead landlords using the name to celebrate the beheading of Charles I. Originally known as the Bull, the pub was the King's Head by 1617, with 31 houses nearby. In 1868 it became the headquarters of the first English cross-country race, the Thames Hare and Hounds. With huge rooms and outside weatherboarding it is a listed building. In 1350 the village was called Rokehampton and meant a home farm occupied by rooks.

## MAYFLOWER, Rotherhithe Street, SE16

Built in 1550 the pub was near the quayside from which the *Mayflower* sailed for America in 1620 laden with Protestants fleeing persecution who

were known as the Pilgrim Fathers. The pub was first known as the Shippe, then became the Spreadeagle and Crown. In World War Two it received a direct hit from a doodlebug causing considerable damage. In 1957 it was restored and named the Mayflower. It is unusual among riverside pubs in that it has its own wharf built on pikes over the river and one can see the water running below. There is a model of the *Mayflower* nearby in the church of St Mary the Virgin. Captain Christopher Jones returned in 1621 to Rotherhythe, died and was buried at this church. It is thought that a boy who sailed with the Pilgrim Fathers composed the lullaby 'Hush a bye baby on the tree top'. He was inspired by the Red Indian custom of putting babies' cradles in the branches of a tree. The *Mayflower*, only 30 metres long and 10 metres wide, had over 100 people below decks. The pub has flagstoned floors with exposed oak beams, narrow settles and small alcove rooms. It was partially built from the timbers of the *Mayflower* when it was broken up.

## MONTAGUE ARMS, Roehampton SW15

An old cottage from the 1700s was converted into a beer house in the 1860s and then became this attractive village pub. By the 1880s it was the stop for the Roehampton to Putney horse buses.

## MORPETH ARMS,
Millbank, SW1

Near the Tate Gallery is the Morpeth Arms, built on an old penitentiary. This 19th-century prison was designed by Jeremy Bentham. (His body was preserved and is at University College, London.) Thames barges were tied up to take prisoners for transportation to the colonies from the prison. An escaped prisoner still haunts the premises – probably on the hunt for a reprieve. Icy chills and noises have been reported. This evil prison went in 1890 and was replaced by an art gallery by Henry Tate. Built into an elegant Regency terrace, the pub was named after chief commissioner, Viscount Morpeth, who redeveloped the area from the stews and slums it was. The whole area was the marshes of west London until Thomas Cubitt found a way to drain it. Among customers now there are ladies and gentlemen of our secret service, based across the river.

## OLD DAIRY, Crouch Hill, N19

It is worth a visit here just for the dramatic exterior of terracotta with large painted panels showing the workings of a dairy from grazing to delivery. It was established in 1839 and John Hinshelwood has published a history of it through the Hornsey Historical Society.

## OLD NUN'S HEAD, Nunhead Green, SE15

First licensed in the reign of Henry VIII, the pub was built on the site of a nunnery suppressed by the same King. The King's Commissioners went to the Mother Superior and gave her an order of expulsion but she resisted the intruders. During the rumpus in 1534 she was murdered and her head was left

on a pikestaff on the nearby green 'For all to see and tremble at the might of the zealous monarch'. An elm tree in the garden is 400 years old. One tale is that the Mother Superior had been caught kissing the King and was murdered to keep her quiet. In 1971 there was a report of swishing curtains in the saloon bar and a pale-faced nun in black apparel appeared. She was the Mother Superior, Elizabeth Barton, and has appeared several times since. A conference room left unlocked was later found locked and an ancient iron key left in the lock. A locksmith said it would be impossible to lock it with that key because it was so brittle it would snap. Springheel Jack, a South London highwayman, used the pub.

## OLD QUEEN'S HEAD, Essex Road, N1

This was the home of Sir Walter Raleigh that later became an inn. Now it is haunted by a woman in Tudor dress and a small, unhappy little girl weeping. There is a patter of little feet, the swish of a long gown and merry laughter and a woman in Tudor dress is sighted. Each first Sunday in the month there is a curious happening. The doors open and close although no one is about and

there is the sound of footsteps going away from the inn. Queen Elizabeth I stayed here as a guest with the Earl of Essex and her favourite clown, Richard Tarlton. Many Queen's Head signs depicted Elizabeth I. Sometimes she was not best pleased with these portraits and ordered them to be pulled down and burned. This was done by a Royal Proclamation of 1563 and any future designs had to be approved by Her Majesty. There is an original Elizabethan fireplace in the pub.

## OLD SERGEANT, Garratt Lane, SW18

The pub has been known as the Old Sergeant since 1789 when it was mentioned in Edwards's *Companion from London to Brighthelmston* (Brighton). Records show that a licence was held here in 1785 and then went into the estate of Earl Spencer, ancestor of Princess Diana. It has changed little over the years and the coach house doors are still there.

## PLUME OF FEATHERS, High Street, SE18

This was the scene for the last hanging of a child, a boy aged nine for  scrumping plums from a nearby orchard in the 1700s. There were many other hangings at this pub as it was used as a magistrates' and coroner's court. The 300-year-old pub was a prison for men on their way to London for execution. Phantoms still roam and there has been much poltergeist activity. One corner of the pub remains forever cold and an electrician was locked in the cellars despite safety handles on the door.

## PRINCE ALFRED, Formosa Street, W9

This is a Victorian pub that has been left well alone and still has original 1862 fittings including glassed partitions that were a feature of most pubs in those days. Five bars each have their own entrance from the street and are separated

by partitions. Cut-glass windows were all the rage then and there is a tall curved front window here that is a splendid example of the craft. Now a Grade I listed building it is named after Prince Alfred, second son of Queen Victoria, who became Duke of Edinburgh in 1866.

## QUEEN ADELAIDE, Putney Bridge Road, SW18

This opened in 1786 as the Queen's Head when Botany Bay became a penal colony and was renamed in 1830. Queen Adelaide married the third son of

George III in 1804 and he became William IV in 1830. Rebuilt in 1838, the pub had a skittle alley in the garden.

## QUEEN'S HEAD AND ARTICHOKE, Albany Road, NW1

In an elegant row of houses the Queen's Head was named after a sister of Henry VIII and widow of Louis XII of France. She was extremely fond of artichokes and persuaded her head gardener to name his tavern so. It is a long cool bar with wooden stools and an open fire with mustard-coloured tiles. There is much wood panelling, large leaded windows and some seats are keg-shaped in basketry. In a 1700s report it was described as 'A small but picturesque house of public entertainment yclept [called] Queen's Head and Artichoke. Attractions include a long-skittle, a bumble-puppy ground and an abundance of cream, tea and cakes.' (Bumble-puppy was an old form of tennis.)

## QUEEN'S HOTEL, Broadway Parade, N19

One of north London's finest inns, built at the time of late Victorian splendour by John Cathless Hill who also built the Salisbury. Here there is much stained glass and designed ironwork typical of the 1890s. There is one vast bar with a billiard room off, both with high ornate plasterwork supported by pillars. It contains a fine, carved, wooden bar with pillars, an open tiled log-burning fire and old photographs of Crouch End. At the entrance is tessellated marble with the initials QH.

## RED LION, Rocks Lane, SW13

For over 400 years an old coaching inn has stood here on one of the main roads out of London. It was rebuilt in the early 1800s when it was a thatched pub called the Strugglers. This was named after the 'drunkard's cloak', a wooden tub with holes for arms and head, instigated by the Puritans for over-indulgers. In 1889 an aeronaut, C.W. Williams, made a parachute jump from a balloon 5,000 feet above the pub grounds. Nearby is a well-known recording studio and people like the Gallaghers, Victoria Beckham, the Verve, the Rolling Stones and the Prodigy all use the inn when in the area. Once the landlady threw out the Spice Girls for being too rowdy.

## ROSE AND CROWN, High Street, SW19

At the time of the English Civil War this was known as the Rose, the most popular flower name for pubs and used as the national heraldic symbol. Although in London this has always been thought of as a country pub. There were once several rooms but now there is one large one, although it is clear from the panelling and open fireplaces just where these rooms were. The Victorian poet Swinburne lived across the common and frequently walked over to the Rose and Crown. Inside there are rare Victorian prints of old London.

## SALISBURY, Grand Parade, N4

Now here is a fine confection of Victorian opulence, an hotel built in the late

1890s by John Cathless Hill. There is fine ornate brick and stonework on the outside, rising through five storeys to a pinnacle with several sided towers. The main entrance is beautifully tiled with mosaic floors leading into the saloon. Inside this saloon is a stained-glass skylight. There are three main bars around a servery with ornate pillars and mahogany bars. Named after Lord Salisbury it is one of the most finely appointed of north London pubs. The area, Harringay, was known as Haringie in 1201 and Haringesheye by 1243 and meant an enclosure in a wood belonging to a man called Haering.

## SPOTTED HORSE, High Street, Putney SW15

Fuchs revealed secrets of the atomic bomb to the KGB at this town pub. It was

called the Blue Anchor in 1754 and usually the use of blue in a pub name indicated they supported Whiggery. The horse is the most popular animal name for pubs and the wooden carving of a spotted horse was added later as this became the name of the pub. At one time there was a skittle alley here.

## SPREAD EAGLE, Wandsworth High Street, SW18

An eagle with spread wings was the national emblem of the Romans and many pubs are named this. It was first mentioned in 1780 but is known to be much older. It was an important coaching inn for visiting magistrates. The agent of Lord Spencer (ancestor of Princess Diana) met tenants here to collect rents. In 1857 there was a tavern, tea room and large ballroom. Part of the building was a theatre for music halls and the first bioscope cinema in London.

## SUN INN, Church Road, SW13

Opposite Barnes Pond is this 300-year-old former coaching inn with an 18th-century staircase. Bowls were originally played on church greens and then on inn greens and this hostelry has a crown green hidden by a brick wall behind it. In 1922 the landlady tried to turn this into a tennis court but after much local pressure relented and the green, there since 1776, was spared.

## TELEGRAPH INN, Telegraph Road, SW15

In 1796, during the war with France, a telegraph system of poles and painted boards was set up near this old coaching inn off the old Portsmouth Road to warn against invasions. These messages were relayed to Chelsea but sometimes smoke would obscure them and a man had to run all the way. In 1821 a new system of semaphore houses was built but abandoned by 1847. The home guard of volunteers trained on the nearby heath with cudgels, pitchforks and the occasional gun. This delightful country inn was a main staging post and Nelson stayed here.

## VOLUNTEER, Baker Street, NW1

This was once a manor house belonging to the Neville family. One ancestor, Robert Neville, a Cavalier during the English Civil War, fought at the Battle of Naseby in 1645, and still 'lives' here as his ghost is seen on many occasions. He appears in the cellar wearing breeches, stockings and a surcoat. It is close to the reputed home of the literary character, Sherlock Holmes, between 1881 and 1904, which is now a museum. The Volunteer was built on the site of the Neville house that was burned down in a fire that killed all members of that family. The word volunteer in pub names refers to volunteer regiments who went to do battle with Napoleon in France and other wars.

## WARRINGTON HOTEL, Warrington Crescent, W9

One of the most opulent taverns, this was a brothel when owned by the Church of England in the late 1800s. Built in 1859 and refurbished in 1900 it has most outstanding pub architectural features. At the entrance there are two large lamps and the porch and walls are covered in glazed tiles. A magnificent saloon bar has a marble-topped semi-circular bar with a carved mahogany base. It is decorated with much Art Nouveau glasswork set in mahogany and carved cherubs surrounded by exquisite plasterwork. The smaller bar is of elegant stucco and has small, etched-glass windows. Music hall star Marie Lloyd used this pub when quaffing champagne with admirers and is said to still haunt the place. One of her empty glasses still adorns a mantelpiece in the lounge bar. Many years ago a jockey rode his horse at a gallop over the pavement and up the steps to win a £100 bet.

## WHITE HORSE, Parson's Green, SW6

Opened in 1688, the year that John Bunyan died, the White Horse name goes back to the 15th century. It had widespread heraldic use by the kings of Wessex and was the traditional emblem of Kent. It also refers to several guilds,

including the innkeepers'. Rebuilt in 1882 it is part terracotta brick with a white horse on the second floor and a large wine butt outside used as a table. Inside are large leather sofas and pew benches.

## WINDMILL, Clapham Common, SW4

One of the most impressive open spaces in South London, the common is surrounded by roads. The name Clapham comes from a homestead or enclosure near a hill or hills and is first mentioned in AD 880 as Cloppaham, becoming Clopeham by 1086 in the Domesday Book. In 1790 the writer Daniel Lysons refers to it as only 30 years previously being a morass and roads almost impassable. The Windmill dates from 1665, the year of the Great Plague of London, and was named after a commercial windmill standing nearby. One miller, Thomas Cresnah, is referred to in the parish records of that year as being an alehouse keeper. Things changed over the years and by 1789 it was mentioned in *A Companion from London to Brighthelmston* (Brighton) as a coaching inn and a very genteel and good accustomed house. It was also a stop-off for gentlemen and ladies returning from Derby Day and there is a painting of one of those occasions by J.F. Herring hanging in the Tate Gallery.

## WORLD'S END, High Street, N1

There has been a pub on this site since 1778 when Hawaii was discovered by Captain Cook. Once it was called the Old Mother Red Cap, the generic name for an ale-wife because they traditionally wore one. This red cap was Mother Jinny, said to practise black arts and heal strange diseases. She was known as Mother Damnable or the Shrew of Kentish Town. When set up upon by the mob she would appear at her hovel door wearing a huge conical red hat and curse them. The Devil was seen to go into her house one night but not come out and she was found dead in the morning. This is a huge Victorian corner pub near a fabulous street market.

# INDEX OF
# PUB NAMES